AF483609

GOD'S
LOVE NOTES

By

Cecilia D. Porter

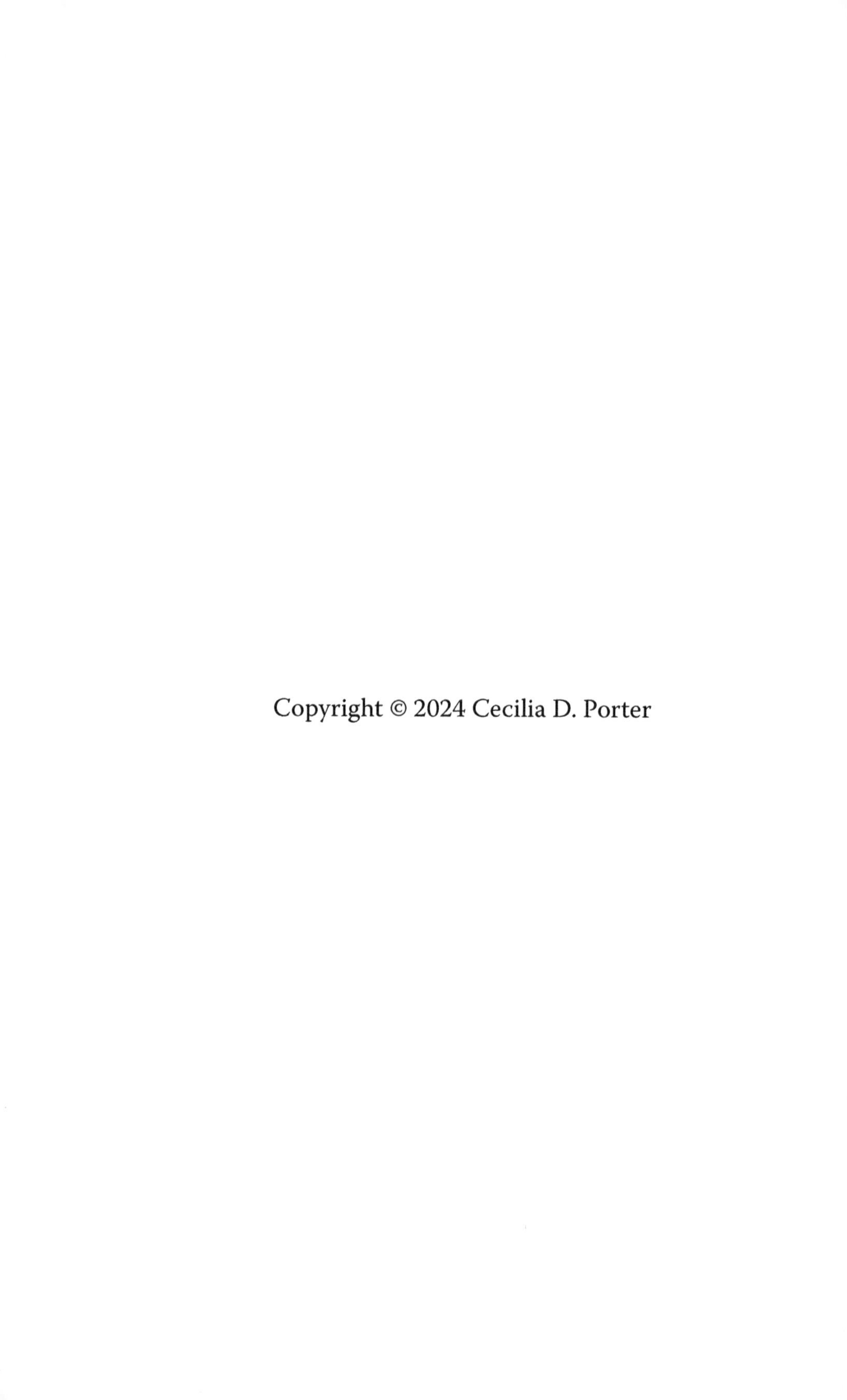

Contents

GOD'S LOVE NOTES

Scriptures about love and God's love for us.

The word L.O.V.E. consist of four little letters. Love is a very short word and it is very powerful. Love is the most powerful thing in the world. Love is also the most powerful weapon in the world. Besides Psalm 91, which discuss the security of the one that trusts in the Lord, 1 Corinthians 13 represents the excellence of love and it is one of the most well known passages in the Bible. This one chapter has become famous as the Love Chapter. The Apostle Paul used the word "love" over eight times in such a short chapter.

Jesus is all about LOVE. The cross of Christ Jesus is the defining act of love. LOVE is central to Christianity. If you were given one word to describe Jesus, what would that word be? LOVE! Jesus told His disciples, "I am the Vine, you are the branches. If a man remains in me and I in him, he will bear much fruit; apart from me, you can do nothing" (John 15:5). In other words, Jesus is saying that when you join me and I with you, then the harvest will surely be abundant. Jesus is the life source that flows from the vine to the branches which produces the fruit. That fruit has the refreshing flavor and aroma of LOVE. We as believers in Christ

have within us His Holy Spirit and that makes us connected to the Vine. The Life Source or the Holy Spirit within us is LOVE.

Jesus love does not fail. Jesus qualifies His love for us, because He tells us especially what He means without ambiguity. Jesus is completely devoted to us. He doesn't hold nothing back and He gives of Himself without any reservation. John 15:13 tells us, "Greater love has no one than this, that he lay down his life for his friends." This is the very best way to love. Love holds nothing back; love willingly gives to a friend. This is what it is for the love of Jesus to be at work in you.

God's love is completely unconditionally and infinite. The Bible gives us a compilation of God's Words so that we could know more about HIM. I would like to share 100 Bible verses that teaches us about love and especially God's love.

1. - John 3:16

"For God so loved the world that he gave his one and only Son, that whoever believes in him shall not perish but have eternal life."

God loves the world so much that He sent His son down from heaven to die for a sacrifice for our sins. There was a debt that needed to be paid, but we could not pay it. So Jesus took it upon Himself and paid the price we deserved to pay. He took on our sins and made a way for us to have the full life that He created for us. Jesus didn't come to condemn the world, but to save the world. Anyone that believes in Jesus Christ as God's Son will be saved. The Son of God, Jesus, came and died for us human beings and the belief in this reality will guarantee you eternal life. Jesus left his throne in heaven to come and show us how deep the love God has for us. The Bible says that the wages of sin is death. In God's mercy, Jesus died in our place.

God loves us so intensely that He could not give us nothing but the absolute the best that He had to offer, so He gave Himself, in the person of Jesus Christ, His Son. What greater love is there? He loves us so much that He died for us. The Bible says that the wages of sin is death. In God's mercy He sent His Son and Jesus' death was costly. It was Jesus through whom and by whom and

for whom all things were created. It is Jesus who is seated at the right hand of the Father in heaven. It is Jesus whom every knee shall bow and every tongue will confess that He is Lord. It is Jesus that has given us access to the throne of grace. It is Jesus who is the King of kings and Lord of lords. The Son of God, the alpha and omega, the One who was and is and is to come, the Messiah, the Christ. Jesus is our Savior and He is our God.

2. - Romans 5:8

"But God demonstrates his own love for us in this: While we were still sinners, Christ died for us."

The love of God was poured out on us like a powerful cascading waterfall. His divine love was displayed in the atonement of our sins, because without the atonement, we would receive Divine wrath. Because of His Divine love for us sinners, He develop an eternal purpose to redeem us, for He sacrificed Himself as a display of God's love. In order to bless humanity, there was no other way to carry out His purpose, but to give His life. His death was a means to an end, because there was no other way, so when He died, He died for us.

Jesus died in our place, because of our sins. God demonstrates His love to the ungodly and sinners. Even before we were born, Christ knew that He had to die for sinners. God came to give us life and life to the fullest. God is the One who justifies and only Christ is sinless. Only He was a worthy sacrifice for our sins. God the Father loves us so intensely that He could not give anything less than His absolute best He had to offer so He gave himself in the person of Jesus Christ, His Son. He showed His love for us, not in an ordinary way, but a supreme way. He showed us His love for us in the death of Christ. What greater love is there? We were loved enough by God that he died for you and me.

3. - 1 John 4:8

"Whoever does not love does not know God, because God is love."

God is love. Not only does God love, but love is who He is. God loves us unconditionally, with an uncommon love. Eternity lies with the compass of that little word, LOVE. God is perfect in love and all His affections are pure and clear. The universe would and could not exist without love, because it is the construct of love.

God's love is our life-line. His love is our guide. We can rely on God's love for us. God's love is unwavering, unconditional, faithful, and it is forever unending. Genuine love can not be exhibited in a community unless if reflects God's love. God's love helps us to be selfless, especially in a self-centered world.

4. - John 16:27

"No, the Father himself loves you because you have loved me and have believed that I came from God."

The Father loved you as well, and as much as the Son does, without any merit or motive in you. He loves us from everlasting to everlasting, and have provided proof, in the gift of His Son to us, and for us. God loves the world and proved that through the gift of His Son at Calvary, and clearly God loves believers of His Son as well.

God's love is not static or unchanging. It is a growing experience in our relationship with the Lord, but He also loves the obedient believer in an especially intimate way. Also, God rewards obedience. When a believer is obedient, Jesus will reveal more of Himself to him or her. God will often use troubling times to draw us closer to Him so that we can experience a more deeper experience of His love for us. So when this happens and we are faced with challenges, we are to allow the suffering in our lives for God to take us where we need to be or where we must go, to experience the fullness of God's love for us.

5. - Jude 1:21

"Keep yourselves in God's love as you wait for the mercy of our Lord Jesus Christ to bring you to eternal life."

We must make every attempt to reman within the protected sphere of God's never ending love as we abide in Christ Jesus and He in us. To stay within the boundaries of God's love, really means to live close to him and not to listen to false teachers who would pull you away form Jesus. When we keep ourselves in God's love, we are clothed daily in His love and are protected by God's armor. We are covered completely in Christ's own righteousness and surrounded by His peace. As we live for Christ's glory and wait in hope for His return, we know that we will our in life eternality with Him.

We are to fight the good fight of faith and keep ourselves in God's love. We must study the Word of God and live a godly life in Christ Jesus our Lord. We must always pray in the spirit and in truth, because prayer nurtures us, it feeds our souls, it keeps us in fellowship with our Father, and it helps us quench all those fiery darts of the wicked one, that every child of God needs for the battle we face everyday.

6. - Psalm 36:5-7

"Your love [mercy], O Lord, reaches to the heavens, your faithfulness to the skies. Your righteousness is like the mighty mountains, your justice like the great deep. O Lord, you preserve both man and beast. How priceless is your unfailing love! Both high and low among men find refuge in the shadow of your wings."

David begins this psalm with a message from his heart as he express how great God's love, faithfulness, and righteousness is for both man and animals. God is loving, faithful, just, and wise. His love is greater than the heavens, which means that God's love, is shown through His mercy, and is very exalted; to the very heavens, as high as the highest object of which man can conceive. His faithfulness reaches past the clouds, which means that His truthfulness, His fidelity to His promises can never be broken. His righteousness, that is His justice. His justice is as solid as a mountain, and His decisions are as full of wisdom as the oceans with water. His justice is His laws; His justice is His providential dealings; His justice is in His plan of delivering man from sin; His justice to the universe in administering the rewards and penalties of the law.

God preserve both man and beast, which means God savest them from destruction. Everyone, man and beast is dependent upon God, to provide our needs, for protection from danger, and His wonderfulness of His Providence. God's unfailing love is priceless, which means no amount of money would purchase those feelings. It is priceless. No amount of money could ever purchase God's love. God's love is a love that we can always depend on and that is why it is one of the reasons that it is priceless. God allows all men refuge in the shadow of His wings, which means the wings of God are wide-spreading and there we can find satisfaction, safety, joy, life, and light.

7. - Psalm 109:26

"Help me, O Lord my God; save me in accordance with your love."

We will all face some difficult times in life and it is a common occurrence for so many people. As we go through those difficult times, some of us will seek help. Some will seek help from a friend, church clergy, or whoever you feel that you can trust. We often cry out to God to help us and what we desire is for God to remove us from the situation or the person that is causing the difficulty. The Bible tells us to cry out to God for help in our challenged times. You will have those difficult times in which you will need God's help. God is full of love, grace and mercy. Because of God's great love for you, God will help you, but maybe not in the way that you think He will.

Sometimes God may delay His help for us. We find ourselves asking the question, "Why is God delaying?" or "What is God doing?" The fact of the matter is, God does not delay at all. God's timing is perfect as all of His ways are. What appears to be a delay to you is actually God working out His perfect plan for you. Don't worry, God will truly help you, because His love for you compels Him to help you.

8. - Zaphaniah 3:17

"The Lord your God is with you, he is mighty to save. He will take great delight in you, he will quiet you with his love."

One thing that you need to know most definitely, God has always been and always will be deeply involved in our lives, no matter what. God is always with us and we are promised that He is ALL-POWERFUL and He is ALL-MIGHTY. God has promised us that He will never leave us nor will he ever forsake us. Whenever we need Him we can call on Him at anytime and any where, whenever, wherever, and for whatever, and He will be right there with us. We are never out of His sight. Whatever we are going through, He is mighty to save us.

He takes delight in you so no matter what you have done, no matter where you are in your walk of faith, He delights in you, because He loves you. Only in God's love we can truly have peace and rest. Whenever you are feeling overwhelmed or anxious, please remember the love that God has for you, and in His perfect timing, He will help you find rest.

9. - 1 John 4:7

"Dear friends, let us love one another, for love comes from God. Everyone who loves has been born of God and knows God."

Let us Love one another
For LOve is from God
EVeryone who
LovEs has been born of
God and knows God.

The word love, dominates much of John's writing. John is identified throughout the New Testament as "the disciple whom Jesus loved," and in his writing is one of the most famous verses in the Bible: "For God so loved the world that He gave His only begotten Son, that whoever believes in Him should not perish but have everlasting life" (John 3:16). Love was the new commandment that Christ gave His disciples. I am pretty sure that as Jesus' disciples spent time with Him, they experienced the love of the Father that was poured out through His Son Jesus Christ. They felt it in the power of the Spirit of God, through the Holy Spirit. Can you imagine how they witnessed the pure essence of God and His character of LOVE? LOVE is the sum of who God is. It is the very nature of God.

We are truly loved by God. God's love is a passion expressed in His action. God expressed His love for us by sending His Son Jesus to live among us and to die for us. And God continues to show us His love. How? Through the gift He gave us, the Holy Spirit. The Holy Spirit confirms it, because once you accept Jesus as your personal Savior, in your heart and in your life, the Holy Spirit comes to dwell in you. He never leaves. He cannot. The Holy Spirit continues to confirm God's love for you. God's love is more truth than the ground we walk on. God's love is so amazing and is totally immeasurable.

10. - Galatians 2:20

"I have been crucified with Christ and I no longer live, but Christ lives in me. The life I live in the body, I live by faith in the Son of God, who loved me and gave himself for me."

To be a Christian is to be a follower of Christ. In what sense have you been crucified with Christ? God looks at it as if you have died with Christ, because your sins have died with Him and you are no longer condemned. You have become one with Christ. Your Christian life began when you died to your old self. Because you have been crucified with Christ you also have been raised with him. In your daily life you must continue to fight against sin. You have been crucified with Christ to the point where it is no longer you who lives but Christ lives in you.

In our walk of salvation by faith, we live by faith and not by sight. Every day of our lives we are trusting in Jesus, as we live by faith in God's Son. It is not enough to have faith in Jesus, to just believe He existed and He died our our sins. No! The faith that we need is the faith of Jesus, the very faith that Jesus had. That means we are to live by everything He did and taught, and this includes abiding by God's rules and laws. Please let's not forget that Jesus willingly died for us and that was His ultimate expression of love for us. Jesus emptied Himself of His divine prerogatives and

became Jesus in the human form then He gave Himself for you and me. And this was all to fulfill God's plan to redeem us from our sins. Our sins have history and the list of all of our transgressions that we have committed or will commit was transferred to Jesus.

11. - Jeremiah 31:3

"The Lord appeared to us in the past, saying: 'I have loved you with an everlasting love; I have drawn you with loving-kindness."'

God reaches toward His people with lovingkindness - kindness that is motivated by a deep love. God is eager to do the best for us, if only we will allow Him. God is constantly reminding us about sin, but God has a magnificent love for us. We may often think of God with fear, but if we look carefully we can see Him lovingly drawing us toward Himself.

God's love for us never subsides nor does it decrease. The love that God lavishes on us is His immeasurable riches of His grace. This means that we cannot earn His love and we could not earn it even if we even tried. God's "everlasting love" is perhaps the most underserving gift that we receive from Him. The fact is, He chose to give us His never-ending love before we were even born.

12. - John 15:13

"Greater love has no one than this, that he lay down his life for his friends."

Agape love is the fatherly love of God for humans, as well as the human reciprocal love for God. It is a selfless, sacrificial love. It is the love of God that allows us to see through the cross of Jesus Christ. It is the love that extends beyond emotions. It is a love that is active and it is demonstrated through actions.

A greater degree of this love has never existed in the world; "that a man lay down his life for his friends." Love in God's kingdom goes beyond anything that the earth can offer. The love of God is perfect and Jesus Christ showed us what perfect love is, by His death on the cross for us. And because of Jesus' sacrifice for our sins, we are called to love our sisters and brothers the same way.

13. - Psalm 86:15

"But you, O Lord, are compassionate and gracious God, slow to anger, abounding in love and faithfulness."

God is full of compassion, grace and mercy, in the most affectionate and tender way. Think of the love a mother has for her child. God loves us far more greater than our parents. God is rich and plenteous in His mercy, and He bestows it freely. God is gracious and so has He been in all eternity. It is proven by His election of grace, by His covenant of grace, and through the provisions in His Son. How? He manifested His kindness in Jesus, from His justification, adoption, pardon, and salvation of his people, and it was all out of grace.

It is God and God alone that possesses almighty power and infinite love. It is through Christ, who is the way, the truth, and the life. Every believer of Jesus Christ should have a desire to be taught the way and the truth of God. It is God who can deliver us from all earthly distress. When the enemy throws those fiery darts at us, we are protected, because God is our Refuge. Jesus is our anchor, even in the middle of the eye of the storm. The compassion, mercy, and truth of God, will be our refuge and consolation.

BE LOVE
We still heard
WE ARE THE ONES WE'VE BEEN WAITING FOR.
Be A PART of the SoLution "That MEANS You too!!"
UBUNTU ALWAYS. One Love.
Justice 4 Shaine Evans
Stay Strong. Love each other!
STAND UP WITH AND For EACH OTHER
I WILL CHANGE THE THINGS I CANNOT ACCEPT
LOVE + LIGHT
Trump's hate
Freedom and Love
SUS
HATE! STOP THE VIOLENCE! Trump
Everyone will be alright ♥
Most HATEst MAN in world
be proud to be YOU!!!!
Live to love!
Now that its done - Lets move forward as 1
I am grateful for you
2018 TURN THE TIDE
We are still here!
PLEASE ♥ ♥ ♥
NESS
American too!
Connection
YOU ARE ENOU
President of the United States of america
the good message are important but do not forget Trump is dangerous Do
The Sun will come

GOD is ALL THERE IS!

I LOVE THE diversity of MY NEIGHBORHOOD ♥ OAKLAND

Inspire

another

Breathe in — PEACE breathe out LOVE

Extreme vetting for Repubicans.

Do all the good you can for all the people you can for as long as you can.

LOVE is LOVE is LOVE

BIG + FROM FRAN

Don't lose heart. We need you ♥ ...E YOU.

Separation of ...s !!!

Where there is ♥ There is life.

LOVE for the possibility of change! ♥

Diverty is Beautiful UNITY

With love and solidarity ♥

We are ONE people

We will Be OK

Love Trumps Hate

Be Active

UR STRONG, YOU CAN GET TRU...

Go Cali...

I Love You

...VE TRUMP HATE!

BLACK

BOO TRUMP

SELF LOVE IN EACH OTHER

14. - Deuteronomy 7:9

"Know therefore that the Lord your God is God; he is the faithful God, keeping his covenant of love to a thousand generations of those who love him and keep his commands."

God is all and in all. There in only one Lord God. "The LORD your God is God of gods and Lord of lords, the great God, mighty and awesome" (Deuteronomy 10:17). God is our sovereign, reigning God. Jehovah is the true God, the faithful God, who keeps His covenant, showing mercy to those who love Him. Faithful means something that can be leaned on or build on. He is a faithful Creator and He is bound to take care those whom He has made. He is bound to supply our needs, to satisfy our desires. Because of His divine nature, He is inexhaustible in power and unchangeable in purpose.

Promises are made and promises are broken. We as human beings have experienced the letdown of a broken promise. What a comfort to know that when the Father makes a promise, He keeps all of His promises. God is faithful to His covenant, and will show mercy and do good to those that love him. God's faithfulness does not waver. He will keep every promise He has made.

15. - 1 John 4:18

"There is no fear in love. But perfect love drives out fear, because fear has to do with punishment. The one who fears is not made perfect in love."

There is no fear in love. There is no room for fear in love. Fear is a natural response to challenges that are unknown to us. Fear can paralyze you or propel you into a frantic behavior. The Bible commands us to not be afraid. As Christians, we do not need to fear, because we know that God is in control. He alone has all power and all authority over everything on the earth, above the earth, and under the earth. "God has not given us the spirit of fear, but of power, and of love, and of a sound mind."

Love is not an affection which produces fear. If you have perfect love in God and to God, you should have no fear of anything. I know it is better said, than done. But there are somethings that we dread. But as Believers in Jesus Christ, we should have no fear of death, for there is nothing to dread. Someone that fears is not made perfect in love. As children of God, we must understand God's love for us. We must understand that we are in God, and God is in us, and that we know that God's everlasting life is in us and by knowing this, we should have peace.

16. - Ephesians 2:4-5

"But because of his great love for us, God, who is rich in mercy, made us alive with Christ even when we were dead in transgressions - it is by grace you have been saved."

The Bible makes it clear that every one of us are sinners and the justice we deserve for our sins is death. Thanks to our Lord and Savior, Jesus Christ for God's grace, mercy, and love, that we don't get what we deserve. It is only by His grace, mercy, and love that we received the invitation of salvation. For Ephesians 2:4-5 clearly tells us that we are sinners that was made acceptable by God's grace and because of His love. God is rich in mercy, which means mercy is not getting what you deserve. God's mercy is another expression of His love. God's greatest mercy is the forgiveness of sin. Your sin debt is paid through the mercy of God. His mercy opens the door to His presence.

Since mercy is God not giving us the punishment we deserve, then grace is God giving us blessings that we don't deserve. God is gracious. It is God's grace that allow His love be put in action. Grace is the favor of God. Grace is getting what you don't deserve. It was God's grace that allowed Jesus to pay the price for our sins. The work of salvation cannot be obtained by our works. No, we

can't earn it. The process of salvation is an act of God's goodness and His unmerited favor. The God we serve is full of grace and mercy. He has a great commitment in loving you.

17. - 2 Thessalonians 3:5

"May the Lord direct your hearts into God's love and Christ's perseverance."

The word "direct" comes from two words: to make straight and down. The idea is to clear away any obstacles in our hearts that impedes our spiritual progress. We must direct our hearts toward receiving instructions from God. Jesus is our beloved Shepherd and we are His sheep. He doesn't lead us without directions. He knows where He is leading us. He is guiding us and the place where He wants to lead us is toward God's love.

For those who have found their eternal salvation in Christ, you need to understand that God will direct each of our hearts into the love of God, so that in Him we will reflect His patient and steadfast love, as we conform, day by day, into the image of Christ. There is no other secure place or situation as being cover by Jesus' abundant and never failing love. God's grace is sufficient and His love is never-ending.

18. - Ephesians 3:17-19

"So that Christ may dwell in your hearts through faith. And I pray that you, being rooted and established in love, may have power, together with all the saints, to grasp how wide and long and high and deep is the love of Christ, and to know this love that surpasses knowledge - that you may be filled to the measure of all the fullness of God."

Faith is all about the heart. God kind of faith is of the heart. The Bible clearly tells us, "For we walk by faith, not by sight" (2 Corinthians 5:7). When you confess Jesus as your personal Savior, you are given the gift of faith. When you have faith in your heart, you must believe not from your mind nor your body. Because thinking is from the mind, but believing is from your heart. When you are rooted and established in love, you are rooted and grounded in the Word of God. God's Word means having a strong foundation in His Word. When you on standing on the Word and wrapped in God's love, whatever trials and tribulations may come your way, you will not be shaken.

God's love is the complete total package. It reaches every corner of our lives in every earthly experience throughout our earthly journey. God's love is wide and it reaches out to the whole world. Race, gender, or social status are all irrelevant to God, because

God's love is wide enough to embrace everyone. God's love is long, as it will continue the length of our lives. It is from eternity to eternity. God's love endures forever. God's love is everlasting and this is the length of God's love. God's love never gives up, it just keep going, and going, and going.

God's love is high. God's love is the highest love, the finest love, the purest love, and not only this, but it is completely free. "Your love, O Lord, reaches to the heavens, your faithfulness to the skies" (Psalm 36:5). God's love is deep and it reaches to the depths of anything that we may go through, including despair, discouragement, and even death. Even through our most difficult situations God's love with be with us, because we are promised that God would never leave us nor forsake us. God's love is deeper than our deepest secrets and God's love is still with us as it peeks into our darkness and our fears. God's love is immeasurable and inexhaustible.

19. - John 15:12

"My command is this: Love each other as I have loved you."

We are to love one another as Jesus loved us, and He loved us enough to give His life for us. We should be motivated to loving others because we love Jesus, and it is the essence of the Christian creed with an extraordinary command of Christ. We should love others in the same manner that Christ loves us. How do we do this? We can demonstrate our love for others by listening, helping, encouraging, and giving. Simply by being genuinely selfless for the sake of others, to family, friends, and even to your enemies. Especially to those that are sick, homeless, those in pain, facing problems, widows, orphans, etc.

You can show your love for others simply by thinking about other people and doing what you can for them so that they are fed, clothed, protected, healed, happy, comfortable, sheltered. Love is from God. If you abide in Christ, then you will live out His love.

20. - 1 John 4:11-12

"Dear friends, since God so loved us, we also ought to love one another. No one has ever seen God; but if we love one another, God lives in us and his love is made complete in us."

The cross is the model for love. The cross is the perfect picture of love, because it is a commitment in the love God has for us. We are called to display the love that was shown on the cross to others and we are to display real love. It is in Jesus, the true model of love that we are to follow. The Scripture says, "We ought to love." The word "ought" is a very interesting word used here, because it indicates a duty or moral obligation. It is used to express justice, moral rightness, or the like. "We also ought to love one another." This is a given purpose that we ought to do - Love on purpose. Love is what we were created to do. If we do not love others, we are denying what we were created to do, because Jesus gave us the perfect model of love, when He died on the cross for us.

No, no one has seen God, but when you show love to others, God abide in you and His love is made perfect in you. Simply put, when you love others and show your love for others, then people are able to see God in you, because God's love is perfected in you. Our job is to faithfully love people that God has given us to love.

21. - Romans 8:35

"Who shall separate us from the love of Christ? Shall trouble or hardship or persecution or famine or nakedness or danger or sword?"

As children of the living King, nothing can keep Jesus from loving us nor separate His love for us. There is absolute nothing we can do to keep Jesus from loving us, and whatever darkness we may face doesn't mean that Christ doesn't love us. Whatever hardship, persecution, trials, trouble, distress, calamities, physical threats or violence we may face, nothing can separate us from Christ's love. Not one of these things means that Jesus does not love us. Jesus reminds us in John 16:33, "I have said these things to you, that in me you may have peace. In the world you will have tribulation. But take heart; I have overcome the world."

Nothing can separate us from Jesus loving us. His love is permanent and Jesus loves us with an unconditional, unadulterated, undying and eternal love. Please understand, no Christian will be able to avoid problems. Matter of fact, no one in this world can avoid problems. No matter what may happen to us, or where we are, we can never be lost to Jesus' love. When we have to suffer, it should not drive us away from God, but we should allow His love to reach us and heal us.

22. - Ephesians 1:5-6

"He predestined us to be adopted as his sons through Jesus Christ, in accordance with his pleasure and will - to the praise of his glorious grace, which he has freely given us in the One he loves."

The word "predestined" means to decree, determine, appoint, or settle beforehand. If you say that something was predestined, you mean that it could not have been prevented or changed because it had already been decided by God. Romans 8:29-30 tells us, "For those God foreknew he also predestined to be conformed to the likeness of his Son, that he might be the firstborn among many brothers. And those he predestined, he also called; those he called, he also justified; those he justified, he also glorified." God is omniscient (knows everything) and omnipotent (all powerful), He has predetermined the fate of all individuals, including their salvation or damnation, before the world was ever formed.

God has adopted us as His own children. Because of His love, God chose us in advance to become His children. The Bible says that we have a choice to choose to believe in Jesus. God will never reject anyone who believes in Him nor will He turn anyone away that is seeking Him. God predestines who will be saved, but you must choose Jesus Christ in order to be saved. God has predetermined that all who are in Christ would be conformed to the image of Christ and adopted as children of God.

23. - Proverbs 3:11-12

"My son, do not despise the Lord's discipline and do not resent his rebuke, because the Lord disciplines those he loves, as a father the son he delights in."

The word "discipline" means "to teach" and "to train." God disciplines those He loves. The purpose of punishment is to inflict a penalty for an offense, the purpose of discipline is to train for correction and maturity. Just like a mother or father discipline their child, God disciplines us when we do wrong. God knows what is best for us. The purpose of God's discipline is not to punish us, but to transform us into the image of Christ. God discipline us to teach and train us. If God did not discipline us, we would find ourselves going down the wrong path, a path of darkness.

God is the source of love. He doesn't punish us because He enjoys inflicting pain on us, but because He is deeply concerned about our development. God discipline us to develop Christian character, to grow in our Christian walk, to become better followers of Him, and because He loves us. God disciplines the ones He loves because He truly do care about us. He loves us and He wants what is best for us. We think that we know what is best for us, but we don't. As God's special children, He will continue to discipline us for the rest of our lives. Although at times, it is very difficult being disciplined, but we must trust God's process and the outcome.

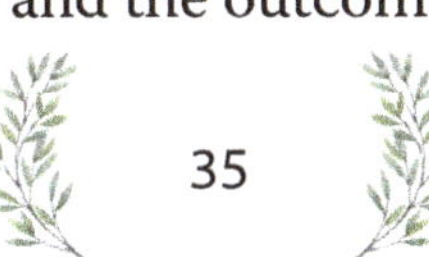

24. - Lamentations 3:32-33

"Though he brings grief, he will show compassion, so great is his unfailing love. For he does not willingly bring affliction or grief to the children of men."

God brings grief within you to bring you to an understanding of what happened. Not only does God understand, but He comforts us during our difficult season. He gives us the strength to persevere. He makes the pain bearable. He soothes those raw emotions. He calms our fears. In this life experience you will experience grief and sorrow, but when that day comes, our hope and confidence can be found in Jesus, because only Jesus can provide you with the strength and comfort you need.

God does not enjoy hurting people or causing them sorrow. He enjoys causing you joy, satisfaction, contentment, and giving us peace, because of His unfailing love. God is that LOVE that passes all understanding. This is the God that gives us strength.

25. - Galatians 5:22-23

"But the fruit of the Spirit is love, joy, peace, patience, kindness, goodness, faithfulness, gentleness, and self-control. Against such things there is no law. "

Those that are in Christ, when they allow the Holy Spirit to lead them, should expect to see the flowing of the "fruit of the Spirit." This is not a list of nine different fruits, but nine single characteristics or qualities of the fruit of the Spirit, as we give God's Spirit control. They do not come in any particular order. Walking in fellowship with the Spirit will yield the fruit of the Spirit. When the singular form of "fruit" is used, it is suggested that the Holy Spirit produces a package of character. The Holy Spirit is the source of the fruit of the Spirit.

The Tree of the Spirit produces good fruits. First there is love. Love is an intense desire to please God, and to do good to mankind. The concept of love is important in loving God, loving others, and even in loving yourself.

Joy is the exultation that arises from a sense of God's mercy that is communicated to the soul. The Bible pairs joy with the Holy Spirit in a way it does not with other affections, because when we experience the Holy Spirit, it empowers joy, and what a difference it makes in our life.

Peace is having the peace of God, "which transcends all understanding." Peace is the harmony and calmness of body, mind, and spirit in trusting in the power and grace of God. Peace is knowing that the Lord is by your side. It is not just knowing it, but also living it.

Patience represents inner strength in the face of adversity, trials, and challenges. It is the ability to endure difficult people and situations without giving into anger or giving up hope. Then there is the patience that is most serious and it is the patience that is required when someone is suffering and it appears that God is slow to answer. We must persevere and be patient when waiting on the Lord.

Kindness is the quality of being friendly, generous, and considerate of others goodness. Kindness is an attribute of love. Kindness is being selfless, caring and compassionate. Kindness is a characteristic of a person's personality. The true main ingredient of love is kindness.

Goodness is the quality of being good, moral, excellence, virtue, kindness, generosity, best part of everything, essence. Goodness is often described as a characteristic of God, that should be embodied by His believers. God is the Source of all than can be called good. God wants us to be full of His goodness. The goodness of Jesus should be demonstrated in our lives everyday.

Faithfulness is a commitment. A commitment is an internal act, an act of heart and mind, of dedicating one's self to something. It is a demonstration of loyalty and trust in God's promises, even when you are faced with adversity or temptation. Faithfulness comes from a place of trust and loyalty. As believers in Christ, it is important to be faithful to God. Faithfulness requires

us to submit our ways to God. We are to faithful to Him and obey His commands.

Gentleness is the quality of being kind, tender, or mild-mannered. Gentleness involves showing humility and thankfulness towards God as well as everyone else. Gentleness is all about how we approach and treat other people. Gentleness does not hate. Gentleness does not insult others, Gentleness puts others first. Gentleness extends grace to others, even the most difficult ones. Gentleness requires a lot of self-control, humility, strength, and thankfulness toward God, with a very polite and kind behavior towards others.

Self-control is the ability to control, to regulate one's emotions, thoughts, and behavior in the face of temptations and impulses, and making decisions of the flesh, and not of the Spirit. Self-control helps us to resist temptation to avoid us from conforming to the things of this world. Jesus Christ is the perfect example of self-control. He lived a sinless life and a perfect life in order to carry out His Father's will. "True self-control is not about bringing our selves under our own control, but under the power of Christ."

26. - Psalm 136:26

"Give thanks to the God of heaven. His love endures forever."

God who is in heaven, is a God who is sovereign, who controls and has power over everything. Every single event is the world is determined by God and God from all eternity, did, by the most wise and holy counsel of His own will, freely, and unchangeably ordain whatever comes to pass. His throne is set in heaven, who is the Maker of it, and the glory of His wisdom and power is displayed. He sits on His throne and keeps His court from whence all blessings come from. This is where He has prepared glory and happiness for His people hereafter; an eternal home in the heavens, an inheritance reserved for the believers in His Son.

The Lord is the One who provides refuge and pursues people to know Him, and the merciful lovingkindness of the Lord has no end. There is no limits on the lovingkindness of God. There are no limits of His time, because He existed before He created anything. There are no limits to His reach, because no matter where you are or what you have done, you could never be out of reach of God's unconditional love.

27. - 1 John 4:19

"We love because he first loved us."

God is love. He isn't just loving, but He is the very definition of love. Our love for God is in response to His love for us. Have you noticed how God's love works? Amazingly, God loved us first. His loved came to us first, then our love responded to His love, then it flowed back to God. God's love is unchangeable and everlasting. How can you love God unless you believe that He loves you? You can absolutely believe it, because God manifested His love to you through the Cross of Jesus. The Father sent the Son into this world and whosoever shall confess that Jesus is the Son of God, God will dwell in them, and them in God. This confession is the foundation of faith that is in the heart, and the acknowledgment of the mouth that Jesus is the Son of God.

God was the Initiator. We did not initiate this love relationship with God, God did. God's love is manifested not by just His feelings, but by His actions. He sent His only Son to earth to live in the midst of human sin and then to die on the cross to be the propitiation for our sins. The word "propitiation" means the turning away of wrath by means of an offering. Jesus offered His own life so that the wrath of God would be turned away from us. God didn't wait to send His Son into this world until we did something

to deserve His love, because if we had to wait until we deserved God's love before He gave it to us, we would have never received it. Jesus loves us with an unconditional, unremitting love. He doesn't need our love to complete Him, He is already completed. He offers us a complete and irrevocable love. He does not love us because we are lovable, but because of who He is, our loving Shepherd.

28. - Psalm 103:8

"The Lord is compassionate and gracious, slow to anger, abounding in love."

The meaning of compassionate is having or showing compassion. It is the feeling or showing sympathy and sadness for the suffering or bad luck of others and wanting to help them. Compassion and mercy is the very character of God. We can take comfort in remembering and knowing that God's compassion is there for us and it will never end.

God is gracious. Gracious is behaving in a polite, kind, and generous way. God is gracious because He is love. Gracious applies to God because of His favor and mercy, His long-suffering, and kindness. It is who He is and His character is to love. God is gracious in our times of need, because it is Him who provides the provisions for us.

God's anger is an expression of his justice and his love for us. But the Bible clearly tells us that he is "slow to anger." Slow to anger means that someone does not become angry easily. They are not easily provoked and generally demonstrate a high level of self-control. So when Scripture reminds us that God is "slow to anger," it means that our compassionate and merciful God is long-tempered, slow to express wrath. When we read about

God's long-suffering, it has to do with His wrath. Does God gets angry? Yes, but it takes Him an extremely long time to do so. Long-suffering is an attribute of God that allows Him to endure our sins as He patiently waits for us to repent, rather than punish us. This is why Scripture reminds us that God's love covers a multitude of sins. God acts with love that is steadfast and dependable.

29. - 1 Corinthians 13:13

"And now these three remains: faith, hope and love. But the greatest of these is love."

The three graces, faith, hope, and love will remain imperishable and immortal. They will remain in the next life for all eternity, exalted and purified. Even in the trinity of graces, there is an order, and love is at the head of it. Faith breeds hope. Nothing can do what faith does, especially the way that faith does it. You cannot have hope without faith. Faith comes first then hope. Faith in God and His Son Jesus is foundational to obtaining eternal life and also for our life's journey here on earth. During the course of your life, as a believer in Christ, you will have to apply strength and power through faith many times. Because faith will carry you through some of the most difficult moments of life.

Hope is a desire accompanied by expectation of or a belief in fulfillment. Hope is commonly used to mean a wish: its strength is the strength of the person's desire. But in the Bible hope is the confident expectation of what God has promised and its strength is in His faithfulness.

Love is the greatest of all human qualities. Without love, faith and hope are nothing. By love you give unselfish service to others, both in things temporal and spiritual. Therefore love is the great-

est because it is most durable. Faith is the foundation and content of God's message, hope is the attitude and focus, love is the action. Love needs faith and hope to survive. When faith and hope are in line, you are free to truly love because you understand how God loves. Love is an attribute of God Himself.

30. - 1 John 4:9-10

"This is how God showed his love among us: He sent his one and only Son into the world that we might live through him. This is love: not that we loved God, but that he loved us and sent his Son as an atoning sacrifice for our sins."

Love originated with God. God is love and we see the greatest expression of His love, by sending His Son. God gave His son as the remedy that offers us a path to redemption that leads to eternal life. Jesus is the image of God in human form. Jesus became the sacrificial lamb, the ultimate sacrifice to saved a sin-sick world from being lost. Jesus' sacrifice was once and for all, both now and for eternity. His sacrifice is for all eternity and His blood provides eternal cleansing. The sacrifice of Jesus shows God's love and His justice.

Love begins with God and ends with God. God's love for us is because of His loving nature and nothing else. We cannot earn it nor do we deserve it. God's number one priority was to display His glory, so He made mankind in His own image to reflect His glory. Because of our sin nature, mankind fell short of reflecting God's glory, therefore He sent His Son Jesus, as the image of the invisible God, and Jesus was the firstborn over all creation.

Yes, the love of God was manifested toward us in the sending of His Son, Jesus. God's eternal love has come for us, and it will last through eternity.

31. - Psalm 91:14

"Because he loves me," says the Lord, "I will rescue him; I will protect him, for he acknowledges my name."

Those that has set their love upon the Lord, being first loved by the Lord, having the love for God in your heart, the Lord will take notice and will be highly please, this leads the child of God to love - to love God. You cannot know God and not love Him. Loving God requires knowing Him, and this knowledge begins with studying His Word, obeying His commands, believing all of His Word, serve Him with all of your heart and with all of your soul, and being thankful for His gifts.

Because of God's loving-kindness, He has a tender concern for His children, and He has made promises to us, that when we call upon Him, He will, in due time deliver us out of trouble. He will rescue us, a deliverance in trouble and a deliverance out of trouble. Whatever calamity may befall God's children, and when we are placed in harm's way, God promises to deliver us, to rescue us, to protect us, and to answer us in time of trouble. All because He says that we know Him by His name and we call Him Father.

32. - 1 John 3:1

"How great is the love the Father has lavished on us, that we should be called children of God! And that is what we are! The reason the world does not know us is that it did not know him."

God has amazing love for us and He calls us His children. As a believer you are not only called children of God, but believers truly are God's children. John 1:12 tells us, "But to all who did receive him, who believe in his name, he gave the right to become children of God." Everyone who believes in Jesus has been born from God. God gives His love to us through His Son, Jesus Christ. The quantity and quality of God's love surpasses all means of comparison and conception, and yet the depths of God's love is immeasurable, incomparable, and inconceivable.

The proof that God loves us is in the gift of Jesus Christ. It was Jesus' death on the cross that displayed a manner of God's love. When you look at the sacrifice Jesus made for us, you see a loved that came from the depth of an Infinite Being, who loves because He must love and who must love because He is God. The Son of Man died for our sins and when you look at the cross, you see the manner of love that the Father has bestowed on us, boundless and endless.

The worldly part of mankind does not know or understand us. They do not understand the reason for our conduct. They do not know or understanding how we can abandon the carnal world for the spiritual world. They do not understand our Christian character and the source of our joy. Because they know Him not. They do not know Jesus nor do they want to know Him.

33. - Romans 5:1-5

"Therefore, since we have been justified through faith, we have peace with God through our Lord Jesus Christ, through whom we have gained access by faith into this grace in which we now stand. And we rejoice in the hope of the glory of God. Not only so, but we also rejoice in our sufferings, because we know that suffering produces perseverance; perseverance, character, and character, hope. And hope does not disappoint us, because God has poured out his love into our hearts by the Holy Spirit, whom he has given us."

We are justified by faith. Justification by faith means that if you are a believer in Christ, you have been justified. This means that God has determined that you are no longer a sinner, because Jesus has covered your sins with His righteousness. Justification is not something that can be earned. There are some amazing benefits that comes with being declared righteous before God by our faith in Christ. The Bible says that grace, life, hope, faith, and the blood of Christ are what justify a person.

When we are justified by faith, we now have peace with God. There is nothing more life changing than the gift of peace with God. Peace with God is different from peaceful feelings such as assurance, security, and confidence. Peace with God means that

we have been reconciled with Him. God never promised us a peaceful life, but He did promise us a life filled with peace, no matter what we may face in life.

In your lifetime, there will be many forks in the road. A fork in the road is a metaphor, based on a literal expression, for a deciding moment in life or history when a choice between presented options is required, and, once made, the choice cannot be reversed. In this Scripture, we are given four forks in the road, suffering, perseverance, character, and hope.

Suffering is listed as the first fork in the road. Paul says that when we have peace with God, we can boast in our sufferings. But this is not so easy to do. But I have learned in my life that God does provides me with His peace when I suffer. Jesus reminds us to cast all of our cares upon Him. Jesus has given us a gift of peace and this kind of peace surpasses all understanding. This peace will give you strength. It will guard your heart.

Perseverance is the next fork in the road. Perseverance is the continued effort to do or achieve something despite difficulties, failure, or opposition. The Christian who perseveres in godliness and spiritual disciplines will be blessed in the very act of persevering. Perseverance is hinged on hope, and faith, and focused on Christ, so when we go through tough times, we will go and grow through the tough times for Jesus' glory. God uses the challenges of the faith race to develop people to be mature and complete in Him. Suffering that is born in faith and trust in God, will produce perseverance.

Perseverance produces character. How? Hardships in our life provides opportunities to develop our character. Challenges makes you stronger and they strengthen your ability to face adver-

sity. Let's say for example, if you desire to run a marathon, you have to keep training everyday despite how difficult it is to do so, that means that you are persevering. When we endure suffering, we must keep our face turned toward God, because the suffering that is endured with trust in God has a way of leading us to a deeper faith in God.

From suffering, to perseverance, to character, to hope. Hope is to want something to happen or be true. It is commonly used to mean a wish: its strength is the strength of the person's desire. But in the Bible hope is the confident expectation of what God has promised and its strength is in His faithfulness. Hope is to trust in, wait for, look for, or desire something or someone; or to expect something beneficial in the future. Hope for sufferers is rooted in the fact that the pain has a purpose. Since suffering has a purpose, then there is good reason to believe that good things will come out of it. The Bible tells us that character produces hope and hope does not disappoint us, because God's love has been poured into our hearts through the Holy Spirit that has been given to us.

We will experience many difficulties in our lifetime that will help us grow. There will be many problems that we will have to face, but those problems will help develop our patience, which will strengthen our character, and that will deepen our trust in God. When you put your trust in God, trust produces obedience, obedience produces hopes, and from hope comes joy and peace. Hope in God is a hope that will never disappoint.

34. - 1 John 4:16

"And so we know and rely on the love God has for us. God is love. Whoever lives in love lives in God, and God in him."

To rely on the love of God means that we must trust Him with our entire being. It is God that knows what is best for us and we must embrace the plans He has for our life. God is the Creator and Controller of the world. We can't control anything. God is always with us and He is our Provider. He even provides us with help in ways that we don't even know we need.

The Bible makes it clear that "God is love." He is the very definition of love. God's love is called "agape." Agape is the self-less, giving, unconditional type of active love. It is the highest and more important form of love. The unfailing love of God for us is part of His covenant with us through Jesus Christ. This means that it cannot be broken and we cannot be separated from God's love.

Whoever lives in love lives in God, and God in him. God wants us to live a life full of love and not just merely live in love, but He wants us to stay in love. When we live a life of love, God is in us and with us. If God's love is in us, we must love others as ourselves. When we abide in His love, we are extending love to all, because God's love is universal.

35. - Ephesians 5:25

"Husbands, love your wives, just as Christ loved the church and gave himself up for her to make her holy, cleansing her by the washing with water through the word."

God gives us a high view of marriage. Here marriage is not a practical necessity or a cure for lust, but a picture of the relationship between Jesus Christ and His church. Marriage is a holy union, a living symbol, a precious relationship. Jesus' love for the church is the model for husbands' love for their wives. The Church is the people, not the building. The Bible says that if you believe in Jesus Christ, then you are God's temple. The Church is all Christians, and the Church is meant to be Jesus' hands and feet.

This Scripture is talking about the duty of husbands to their wives. Husbands, without abuse and oppression, should love their wives, as Christ loved the church. With a love that is pure, constant, sincere, and kind. A true model of affection with loving-kindness. Jesus loved the church and He gave Himself as a ransom. Since such an example has been exhibited, that is the reason for the husband to loved their wife as Christ loved the church. Jesus gives the perfect model for a husband to imitate.

36. - Psalm 13:5

"But I trust in your unfailing love; my heart rejoices in your salvation."

Many storms will enter our life, such as loss, pain, tribulations, trials. It is totally unavoidable living in this sin sick-world. The storms are always unexpected and they throw your life into total turmoil. Life that was once calm and peaceful one minute, then the next minute you are in the midst of something that is life-changing. No matter what storms you may face in your life, Jesus promised us that He will never leave us nor forsake us, because He is able to see us through any storm. After all He is our anchor in the storm. Jesus tells us in John 16:33, "In the world you will have tribulation. But take heart; I have overcome the world." You must have the confidence to trust God completed, no matter the situation or problem.

"My heart rejoices in your salvation," is not referring to the saving of human beings from sin and its consequences. But the word "salvation" here is about God's deliverance from a present trouble or placing you into a condition of safety. There will be a rejoice in salvation when God rescues you from your current state of distress. There is a process sometimes that we must go through. We go from prayer to complaining, from complaining to praying,

from praying to believing, from believing to trusting, not in your-self, but in the mercy of God, in the grace and goodness of God. God is the author and giver of joy and all good things. You have to believe that whatever you are going through, God will get His glory and you will rejoice.

37. - Romans 8:37-39

"No, in all these things we are more than conquerors through him who loved us. For I am convinced that neither death nor life, neither angels nor demons, neither the present nor the future, nor any powers, neither height or depth, nor anything else in all creation, will be able to separate us from the love of God that is in Jesus Christ Jesus our Lord."

In answering a preceding questions, "Who shall separate us from the love of Christ?" The answer is "Nothing" can separate us from the love of God. There is no such powerful thing or person that separate us from God's love. There is nothing that can enter your life that is able to separate you from God's love. His love allows us to be more than a conqueror in any adversity. God walks with us through every adversity we have to face. He is there in every hardship. A conqueror defeats their enemy, and the Bible tells us that we have an adversary "who walks around like a roaring lion, seeking whom he may devour." Whatever the enemy means for evil in our lives, God uses it for our good, because He uses these attacks for His glory and for His purpose in our lives.

No matter what you can list, death, life, angels, demons, powers, height, depth, things present or to come, it is not powerful

enough to separate you as a Believer in Christ Jesus, from the love of God. There is absolutely nothing that can cause God to reject you. God loves you totally and completely unconditionally. No matter how many foes you can enumerate, no matter the various forms of distress you can specify, no matter the numerous evil inflictions for Christ's sake, no matter the physical evils (hunger nakedness, peril or sword), when compared with the love of Jesus, He can shield us from them all.

38. - Isaiah 54:10

"Though the mountains be shaken and the hills be removed, yet my unfailing love for you will not be shaken nor my covenant of peace be removed, says the Lord, who has compassion on you."

God's love is powerful, and yet it is gentle. It is permanent with permanence and it is mightier than anything. The mountains shall depart and the hill be removed, but God's loving-kindness and His covenant of peace shall outlast them all. There is a tender-heartedness of God with an infinite love for His children that can never die. His love and kindness will continue from everlasting to everlasting. Oh what a revelation! God's love that is taller than any mountain, roots that are deeper than any tree, wider than the heavens, His tenderness grasps us, keeps us, and will not let us go. God lavishes His love on us and His love pleads with us, rebukes us, and corrects us when we need correction. Knowing this, what can we say about the tender, changeless love of God? This God of ours that says, "I promise that My love shall never leave thee." He gives us a covenant that is totally irrevocably, forever.

God has made us many promises and one such promise we have is a promise of peace. Peace is a calm state of mind, tran-

quility, and freedom from strife. Peace is a gift from God. He give us this peace through Jesus Christ. God bound Himself by His promise to give us the peace that belongs to Him, and that covenant is sealed to us in the blood of Jesus. There is no peace without Jesus. You know there is a saying that goes: "Know Jesus, Know Peace, No Jesus, No Peace." That is absolutely correct. If you do not have Jesus in your life, then you will have a life full of chaos. Our precious Eternal God longs to bless and love us, with His unchanging love, and faithful covenant of perpetual peace.

39. - John 15:9-10

"As the Father has loved me, so have I loved you. Now remain in my love. If you obey my commands, you will remain in my love, just as I have obeyed my Father's commands and remain in his love."

What an indescribable love! The eternal love of the Father goes forth to the Son, and from the Son it goes forth to all who would receive it. Jesus is telling us that He loves us; deeply, purely, fully, and with a divine affection.

God desires for us to remain in His love and to rely on His love. What awesome, tender affection He has for us. He tells us to remain (abide) in His love and this draws us still closer to Him. He wants us to continue to stay in His sweet and sacred atmosphere of His love.

When we obey God's commands, then we will remain in His love. This assures us that by keeping His commandments, we shall continue to be safe in the stronghold of His love. If you love God your heart will obey, and it obeys because it loves, and it bows to the will of submission to the love for Jesus.

40. - John 13:34-35

"A new command I give you: Love one another. As I have loved you, so you must love one another. By this all men will know that you are my disciples, if you love one another."

Jesus tells us that He gives us a new commandment and this new commandment is to "love one another." If you have love for Jesus and when your heart are in tuned with Jesus' heart, then you will have a love for others. This love defines your faith. It is characterized by selflessness and it has the power to transform lives. With this love, you will care and have compassion for others. This means serving, helping, and caring for others.

As Jesus has loved us, we must love one another, and this simply means, let us not just love in words, but in deed and in truth. When Jesus died on the cross, He was not about pleasing Himself, we saw a self-sacrifice type of love. The Bible clearly tells us, "Greater love hath no man than this, that a man lay down his life for his friends." Jesus have set the pattern for us, and how should our love look like: self-sacrificing and an active love. Always remember, a love language is all about sacrifice.

41. - John 15:12

"My command is this: Love each other as I have loved you."

Jesus wants to emphasize that we should have an unconditional love of God flowing through us and this love should join us together. Jesus' commandment here, means abiding in His love. Your love for God is proved by your love to mankind. We are commanded to love. Love is an obligation that involves everyone, in that we are to be kind and loving to one another. This is a simple commandment given to us, and we are bound to love everyone. Let's not forget that we are the children of God and we are commanded to love our brothers and sisters.

Love is a matter of the heart. When the heart is right your conduct will be right. Love is action. If you say that you love someone, you must show it, you must prove it. Love is just not an emotion that you feel, love is something you do. Love is a feeling that affects your actions. When you look at all the ways God wants us to grow our faith, love is right there with knowing, flowing, and believing.

Love is self-sacrifice. Jesus became the final and complete sacrifice for our sins. He was pierced and punished for our transgressions. Jesus gave His life for us and this was because He loves us. Jesus has provided us the the perfect example of love, so let us imitate the love of Christ.

42. - Colossians 3:14

"And above all these put on love, which binds everything together in perfect harmony."

When the term "above all" is used, it means before every other consideration. Love is above all. Love is all we need and all we need is love. This sounds really simple, naive, and idealistic, but it is almost impossible. But love is the more perfect way, because love is the most supreme attribute. Love supersedes all attributes. To put on love, is a choice to walk in Jesus' love. To put on love you have to put on humility and kindness. When you put on God's love, this becomes the foundation for everything. Love becomes the chain that binds us.

Love is the perfect bond of unity. Love brings people together. It is God's love that binds us together. Love is the greatest bond of unity. Unity is the quality or state of being made one (unification). Unity is impossible without love. Love binds together in perfect harmony and when you put on love, you should be clothing yourself in truthfulness, compassion, kindness, humility, gentleness, and patience. These are virtues and these virtues are all manifestations of love. To love is to be truthful. To love is to be compassionate. To love is to be kind and humble. To love is be be gentle and patient.

43. - Psalm 63:3

"Because your loving-kindness is better than life, my lips will praise you."

God's loving-kindness is in itself better than life could ever be and all the comforts of life could ever offer. In our earthly life there will be a mixture of joy and pain, happiness and sorrow, love and loss, triumphs and setbacks. Through all the joys, gladness, beauty, and all the various pains, suffering, and agony, that you go through in this life, it is the loving-kindness of God that gives us strength to get through all these things. It is that love of God, that is better than life to which we hang on. God's grace and His mercy is far more valuable than life. Life cannot offer no comfort or joy without God's divine favor through His blessings.

Because we experience God's grace and mercy, these exceeds all the blessings of life, and we should open our mouths with praise, glorifying HIm. Praise refers to lifting God up. It is a joyful recounting of what God has done for you. Praise and thankfulness goes hand in hand as you thank God, by showing appreciation for who He is and acknowledging all the wonderful things God does for you. So when you glorify God, you are acknowledging the greatness and splendor of His Majesty through honor, worship, and praise.

44. - Isaiah 41:10

"Fear not, for I am with you; Be not dismayed, for I am your God; I will strengthen you, I will help you, I will uphold you with my righteous right hand."

God wants us to be filled with hope and trust and not be fearful. Fear as a noun means uncountable: unpleasant emotion caused by actual or perceived danger. Fear is a strong uncontrollable, unpleasant emotion caused by actual or perceived danger or threat. When God tells us to "fear not," He is telling us not to worry or to be frightened. We are not to fear, but only believe in His command of protection. Through the Scriptures we can hear His voice encouraging us onward.

Dismay is a sudden or complete loss of courage and firmness in the face of trouble or danger; overwhelming and disabling terror; a sinking of spirits. Dismay is a stronger and upscale "fear" than "afraid." We all are fearful every now and then, but when you are "dismayed" you are so overcome with fear that you become "frozen" or "disabled" by the fear. There is a term that is often use, "like a deer in headlights." This term describes the term "dismay." We become frozen with fear. God wants us to not be dismayed, because He is our God. He will help us, for He is our Redeemer.

God wants us to know that He is our God and all the followers Jesus has power over darkness. God has provided us with His comfort, to supply all of our needs and wants, and answers to all of our prayers. What consolation in knowing with assurance that He is with us to protect us. Our God has all power and that power was pledged for our protection.

God wants His children to know that He "will uphold you with my righteous right hand." God provides us with His divine protection. How? By His supporting, ordering, observing, and by His divine providence, because He is Father over all, who is over everything. God is sovereign, that is He has supreme authority and absolute power over all things. So in His way of providing us with grace, He guards and protect his children, by supporting them, supplying them, comforting them and strengthening them; therefore they need not fear any of their enemies.

45. - Lamentations 3:22-23

"The steadfast love of the Lord never ceases; his mercies never come to an end; they are new every morning; great is your faithfulness."

God gives those that are His a comforting promise, His love will never cease. Scripture reveals God's eternal love for us. Love is an attribute of God's character, it can never leave us. It will remain for all eternity. Love persists against all opposition. It is permanent.

God's mercy is unending. Mercy is compassion or forgiveness shown toward someone whom it is within one's power to punish or harm. God does not put limits on His mercy. God's mercy is just like His love, it is unconditional. His mercies never comes to an end and this means that God is all-forgiving. He is ready to keep giving us another chance, over and over again. The greatest example of God's mercy is Jesus paying our sin debt by dying on the cross for us.

God's gives His mercy toward us everyday. It is refilled and refreshed each and every day. The mercy of the Lord is from everlasting to everlasting. The mercy of God is great. It is sovereign, free, and unchangeable.

46. - Psalm 5:11

"But let all who take refuge in you rejoice; let them ever sing for joy, and spread your protection over them, that those who love your name may exult in you.

When you take refuge in the Lord, by putting your trust in Him, you should expect to rejoice. Favor and joy is bestowed on those who will trust and obey God. To trust in God is to run to Him for refuge, and there you will find peace. As you run to find a hiding place when its dangerous, the soul that trusts in Jesus takes flight to God, because in Him is security and we should rejoice in His protection.

The children of God have every reason to be happy, because we partake in the favor of God. At the same time, we should give an earnest expression for a desire to rejoice. To be joyful in Him. To rejoice in Him. To rejoice in His perfections. Joy is the privilege of the children of God. We should shout joyfully, not just inwardly, but outwardly. Just to think about God should fill our hearts with joy, because He lavish us with His love, and He allows us to see His goodness.

47. - 1 Chronicles 16:34

"Give thanks to the Lord because he is good, because his faithful love endures forever."

Give thanks to the Lord because He is good. We should give thanks to the Lord for everything, and everyday. As a believer, we should be thanking God with hearts full of gratitude. Because God is continually blessing us, protecting us, providing for us, each and everyday. God blesses us every day in so many ways and He lavish us every day with His grace and mercy. A day should not go by without us, from our hearts, expressing our gratitude to God for our life and the very air we breathe.

God is so very good to us. God is good all the time. God is omnipresence, that means that God's presence is inescapable and that He is "everywhere present." God is always with us and He never changes. He is always the same, because He is always graceful, faithful, protecting, and loving.

God's loves never changes that is why His love endures forever. God is Love and it is a love that is rooted in forgiveness. It is a love that has no end. God's love is possessive. God's love is called agape, which is the highest and purest form of love.

48. - Psalm 107:8

"Let them give thanks to the Lord for his unfailing love and his wonderful deeds for men."

We should give thanks to the Lord for His unfailing love, His great love and how He has shown His love to us. God gives us reasons to thank Him by how He has delivered us by His great love, and how Jesus backs this up. How? We, the redeemed, were once lost, and we could not have possibly found our way without Jesus. We were once thirsty and hungry, physically and spiritually running on empty. Then Jesus told us, "I am the bread of life. He who comes to me will never go hungry, and he who believes in me will never be thirsty" (John 6:35).

We must thank God for His wonderful deeds for us, because of His great love for us, He came and rescued us from the flames of hell. He saved us from ourselves. Jesus is our Redeemer. To redeem something is to pay a price to win it back. Jesus set us free by paying the price with His own blood that was shed on the cross. Through Jesus Christ, God has provided us help through the storms of life and He guides us to safety. So when we cry out to God in trouble and distress ("God, please help me"), He hears us and He calms the storm and bring peace into our lives.

49. - Romans 8:31-32

"So what are we going to say about these things? If God is for us, who is against us? He didn't spare his own Son but gave him up for us all. Won't he also freely give us things with him?"

If God is on your side, then who can possibly stand against you? There is no one that can bring condemnation against a believer. Who could bring a charge against God's elect? God is always working on our behalf, and nobody can really do anything against us. We have been chosen as His children and we are His heirs. God foreknew us. He predestined us, called us, justified us, and has glorified us. Then you must know that He is for us. And if God is for us, then who can be against us?

God loves us so much that He sent His own Son to die for our sins, and this same God will give you the grace and strength that you will need to handle every trial. God did the greatest thing for us when He sacrificed His own Son. Since He didn't even spare His own Son for us, how will He not freely give us all things? Why would He not supply us with all that is needed for godliness and life? In God's great love for us, He gave His beloved Son, in whom He was well pleased.

Not only was Christ given for us, but Christ was also given to us. Since He was given to us, He will surely gives us all things, all things that He sees to be necessary and needful for us. He will give us all good things. Freely giving freely, without reluctancy.

50. - Psalm 109:21

"But do thou for me, O God the Lord, for thy name's sake; because thy mercy is good, deliver thou me."

"Do thy for me." What shall He do? Lord do whatever You think is best for me. This is leaving everything in God's hands and waiting for God to answer your prayer. You must completely rely on God to do what is best for you, not trusting in what it looks like, but by faith believing and trusting in the One who is able to demonstrate His power in some unbelievable way.

The phrase "for thy name's sake" means showing God's abilities and His character. It's for the sake of God demonstrating His character. God has a mighty great name and His name extols His character, His integrity, His reputation, His glory, and His holiness. God often acts to sanctify and protect His holy name. If God is for you, who could be against you. If God is for you, He will do exceeding, abundantly far more than you are able to ask or think. Whatever you may be going through you can truly come before the Father, and by asking in Jesus' name, allowing God to exert His power on your behalf.

"Because of thy mercy," and His mercy is good. The loving-kindness of God is shown through His mercy. This is a quality that shows His compassion, His forgiveness, His kindness and His

true love for us. His mercy endures forever. But no one can earn God's mercy. By definition, "mercy" is something given to those who do not deserve it nor cannot earn it.

"Deliver thou me," and He will deliver you from the challenges, troubles and problems that you face. No matter where you are spiritually and no matter what you may be struggling with, God understands, and He is able to help you. Only He can calm the raging storm in our lives. He can replace the bitterness and despair with joy and peace. He can repair what is broken in our lives. He wants nothing more than to strengthen and comfort us.

51. - Micah 7:18

"Who is a God like you, pardoning iniquity, overlooking the sin of the few remaining for his inheritance? He doesn't hold on to his anger forever; he delights in faithful love."

There is only one true living God. God is three persons in one. The holy Trinity is God the father, God the Son (Jesus), and God the Holy Spirit. God is so mighty and so great. He is majestic in holiness, awesome in glorious deed, and He is the ultimate authority over all things.

It is God and only God that can pardon iniquities and forgive sins. Iniquity is a type of sin that includes a conscious decision to hurt someone else or to rebel against God's law. Iniquity is characterized by wickedness or immorality, primarily referring to the nature and character of an action rather than the action itself. The term sin is used to describe any act, thought, or attitude that falls short of God's perfect standard of righteousness. So because of the perfections of God's nature, we receive the blessings of His goodness, both of providence and grace, as He lifts up and take away our iniquity and sins off of us and have laid them on Jesus Christ, and He has bore them, and has carried them away, never to be seen and remembered any more.

God delights in those who loves Him, who places their hope in Him, and trust Him. The word delight means to gain great pleasure, satisfaction, and happiness. God delights in you simply because of who you are. You are His child and He loves you.

52. - Romans 8:28

"We know that God works all things together for good for the ones who love God, for those who are called according to his purpose."

God has made a promise. What is the promise? As a child of the living King, those who are saved, "all things will work together for good." "All things" no matter the circumstance, every circumstance you might experience, every pain, suffering, trials, tribulation, will be worked out for our good. God is always there for us, with power and passion, for those He loves, even when our human eyes do not see it. But you must understand that when God is working "all thing together for good," the "good" is from His perspective and not ours. God uses "all thing" for good, even the bad and unpleasant things.

For those that loved God, God will make your sufferings work for good if you love Him. Jesus clearly tells us," If you love me, you will obey what I command." Loving God will include obeying all of His commands. In the Bible Jesus tells us how to love God: "Love the Lord your God with all your heart and with all your soul and with all your mind" (Matthew 22:37). God desires for us to have an intimate relationship with HIm. Our love for Him is a response to His love for us.

What does it mean to be called according to His purpose? It means that you have been called according to the purpose of God. What is this purpose? Before the beginning of the world, God knew who He would choose to receive His free gift of salvation. God's purpose for us was not an afterthought, because it was settled before the foundation of the world. God has always known who would be saved and who would not. "For these whom He predestined, He also called; and these whom He called, He also justified; and these whom He justified, He also glorified" (Romans 8:30).

53. - John 14:21

"Whoever has my commands and obeys them, he is the one who loves me. He loves me will be loved by my Father, and I too will love him and show myself to him."

We show our love for Jesus by obeying Him. Our true love to Jesus will produce obedience. By keeping Jesus' commands is a proof and evidence the you love Him, not just in word only, but in deed and in truth. By keeping Jesus' commands is a test of our love for Him. It is a steady obedience, by walking in His ways, as a true believer. Being obedient to God means that we trust and respect Him and we are truly believing that He knows what is best for us.

If you love Him, then you will obey what He commands. Those who loves Jesus will be loved by the Father and this shows that there is a union between the Father and the Son. Jesus gives a special kind of love to all believers. This special love of Jesus will be followed by the special love of the Father. God will take pleasure in loving the believer.

By loving Jesus, He will show Himself to us. To show Himself is to make an appearance, to place before the eyes so that an object may be seen. This means that Jesus will show Himself not in a visible way, but in a spiritual manner, in the consciousness of the soul. Jesus will take special measures to disclose His Person and goodness to us.

54. - 1 Corinthians 13:4-7

"Love is patient, love is kind. It does not envy, it does not boast, it is not proud. It is not rude, it is not self-seeking, it is not easily angered, it keeps no record of wrongs. Love does not delight in evil but rejoices with the truth. It always protects, always trusts, always hopes, always perseveres."

Jesus gives us the "Great Commandment," He tells us that the most important thing we can do is to love God with all of our heart, our soul, our mind, and our strength. Then He tells us secondly, to "love our neighbor as you love yourself."

Love is patient means that love and patience are products of the Spirit's presence in your life. Love is patient because God is patient and love cannot exist without patience. Love is patient. Love is not impatient. The word patient means to be able to accept or tolerate delays, problems, or suffering without becoming annoyed or anxious.

Love is kind. Kindness is the quality of being considerate, selfless, caring, compassionate, helpful, and unconditionally kind. Kindness is patience in action. Kindness is more than being nice, it is being sincere and doing things intentionally. It is a voluntary act of kindness, doing something without expecting anything from it.

Love does not envy. Selfless love is not jealous. To envy is to feel resentful and unhappy because of what someone may possess or achieved. As a believer in Christ, we are not to carry on like the world, envying and angry about other people's success. We should be happy with the blessings that God has given us.

Love does not boast. To boast is to talk with excessive pride and self-satisfaction about your achievements, possessions, or abilities. If your conversations are centered around you, what you have, how good you are, or your accomplishments, then you are being boastful. Remember, everything that you possess are gifts from the Lord. We should be thankful for everything we have because they are underserved gifts from God.

Love is not proud. Love does not behave in a prideful, snobbish, arrogant, overbearing, insolent manner. God keeps reminding us that real love is not proud. Love is not puffed-up. I am not talking about being proud of yourself, humbly, because many people can pride themselves on something. Maybe you are proud of your work ethnic, or getting healthier, or just a naturally proudness of yourself in some way or another. This is not sinful. We can rejoice and take pride in who God made us to be, and there is no need to be someone else.

Love is not rude. A rude person is ill-mannered, discourteous, or insulting. This type of behavior is inappropriate and isn't very nice. Love displays proper manners. It helps you understand when to act and when to do absolutely nothing. Love helps you understand when to speak and when to remain silent.

Love is not self-seeking. A self-seeking person is a person that is concerned chiefly or only about themselves. They are only con-

cerned about getting what they want or need and they do not care about what happens to other people. Love is not selfish.

Love does not easily angered. Love is not irritable, testy, nor touchy. Love does not easily get upset, offended, or angered. Short-tempered or short fuse is a more formal way of saying that someone gets angrily easily. The Book of James makes it plan, "You must all be quick to listen, slow to speak, and slow to get angry" (James 1:19).

Love keeps no records of wrongs. This means that if you are still keeping records of past offense, you have not truly forgiven the person that you are still holding a grudge against, because you are still keeping records of mistakes and shortcomings of others. Instead, love emphasizes forgiveness and understanding.

Love does not delight in evil but rejoices with the truth. When you embrace the qualities of God's love, then you are honoring God, because God hates all forms of evilness. We should never delight in being comfortable with wrongdoing, because the Bible truly tells us, "Woe to those who call evil good and good evil, who put darkness for light and light for darkness who put bitter for sweet and sweet for bitter" (Isaiah 5:20). God's love rejoices with the truth. What does it mean that God's love rejoices with the truth? It means that it is a love that put others ahead of ourselves. It is a love that sacrifices self for others. We must care for one another, serve one another, and show sincere affections for one another. This type of love is real, sincere, and it honors God.

Love always protects. Love provides a sense of security, a feeling of belonging. It protects. How? It reduces anxiety. Love can also increase activity in the area of the brain associated with the control of pain. Love protects us emotionally. Love protects us

from feeling lonely and isolated. Love provides us with a sense of purpose.

Love always trust. When you trust someone, you believe that they are honest and sincere and will never deliberately do anything to hurt you. Love is not suspicious and doubting of others. Love believes that a person is innocent until proven guilty. It doesn't jump to conclusions. Trust is what it takes for love to flourish. Love sees trust instead of mistrust, because love thinks the best of others.

Love always hope. Hope implies little certainty but suggests confidence or assurance in the possibility that what one desires or longs for will happen. Whenever there is love, there is hope. Even when it seems that there is no reason to hope, love finds the hope. Love continues to hope.

Love always perseveres. Perseveres means to continue making an effort to do or achieve something, even when it is difficult or takes a long time. In our Christian walk, God encourages us to persevere and this denotes the steadfast endurance and resilience, even in the face of adversity, hardships, and challenges. In other words, love never gives up, never losses its faith, and endures through every difficulty, and goes beyond bitterness and betrayal. Love continues during the best of times and in the worst of times.

Love never fails. To fail means not to succeed in what you are trying to achieve or expected to do. Love never fails, but without love, we fail. Love never fades nor does it ends. We as children of God, will be loved forever. Scripture reminds us, "There are three things that remain - faith, hope, and love - and the greatest of these is love" (1 Corinthians 13:13).

Love embraces patience, because it is patient. Love embraces kindness, because it is kind. Love embraces protection, because it protects. Love embraces trust, because it is trustworthy. Love embraces resilience, because it bears all things. Love embraces faith, because it believes all things. Love embraces hope, because it is hopeful in all things. Love embraces endurance, because it endures all things. Love embraces perseverance, because it never fails.

Love resists envy, because it is not envious. Love resist boasting, because it is not boastful. Love resist pride, because it is not prideful. Love resist rudeness, because it is not rude. Love resists self-seeking, because it does not insist on its own way. Love resist anger, because it is not ill-tempered. Love resists keeping records of wrong, because it is not resentful. Love resists evil, because it does not rejoice in wrongdoing.

55. - Psalm 31:7

"I will be glad and rejoice in your love, for you saw my affliction and knew the anguish of my soul.

God loves you and He cares when we are hurting. God is love and He truly loves us with the most deepest type of love there is. God sees your pain and He hears your cries. No matter how much you love Jesus, He loves you so much more. He knows that we will have many trials and sorrows, and He doesn't leave us alone to figure it out by ourselves. His Holy Spirit helps us in our times of struggles. The Bible tells us that the Holy Spirit makes intercession for us with groaning which can not be uttered.

God is omniscience, which means that He is all-knowing. He is omnipresent which means that He is everywhere all at once. He is omnipotent which means that He has all-power. So nothing can escape the all-seeing eyes of God and nothing can happen to you without His knowledge. He sees every temptation and trial that confronts us and He invites every believer to approach His throne of grace in prayer, but prayer and faith must go together. Faith erases any doubt and brings the belief that things will work out.

56. - 2 Corinthians 5:14-15

"For Christ's love compels us, because we are convinced that one died for all, and therefore all died. And he died for all, that those who live should no longer live for themselves but for him who died for them and was raised again."

You see the full circle of God's love, because God demonstrated His love for us through Jesus Christ. He died for all, because of our sin, He died in our place, but He rose again and guarantees us eternal life through His sacrifice. We would all be lost, dead to sin having no power of deliverance, and would remain miserable forever, if Christ had not died for us.

And He died for all. Jesus did not become human to live a life for Himself. He didn't come to this sinful earth to acquire wealth or to enjoy earthly pleasures, or to obtain a reputation for Himself. He lived a life of self-denial and toiling for the purpose of the death of the Redeemer, to be a Savior who died for all. So that they who are Christians would live. The sacrificial atonement was for all, but only a part are made alive to God, because many will reject Him. But He died for all. He not only died for the elect, but for all others. He died to embrace the whole human race. For Jesus died so that mankind will live, live a life of justification, for all those

he died for, for them He rose from the dead to acquit them of their sins.

We should no longer live for ourselves, but for Jesus who died for us. When you live for Jesus it is the opposite of living for yourself. Living for Jesus means that your view of life will changed. You will give up your life and accept the plans that God has for your life. You have to be willing to let go and let God have His will in your life by following Him. When you surrender to Jesus, you will begin to be more like Christ, in our words, opinions, thoughts and actions.

57. - 1 John 3:16

"This is how we know what love is: Jesus Christ laid down his life for us. And we ought to lay down our lives for our brothers."

God gave the His only begotten Son, because He loved the world so much. Jesus sacrificed Himself on the cross for us and it was done out of love. Do you see the miracle, the mystery of God's Divine love? How awesome and divine that God saved us with His own blood. God Himself in His divine nature suffered for us. By this we know what true love is. God's love is powerful, it sacrifices. God's love was seen in its highest form when Jesus gave Himself to die on the cross. God sent His Son from heaven to earth to become a man to die for our sake, so that sinful people would not perish. Jesus lived a perfect life of obedience to God, suffered on a wooden cross for our sins, where he died for our substitution. Because God gave the world His only beloved Son, this should never leave any doubt about His love for us.

Because Jesus laid down His life for us, we ought to lay down our lives for our brothers, if circumstance should require it. Jesus Christ did it for us and we should desire to imitate His example. We should have such love for the church and our fellow believers to be willing to jeopardize our lives to help them. We should have

such a love for the truth to be willing to sacrifice our lives for it rather than deny it. True love was illustrated by Jesus' love for us. We should lay down our lives by giving our time, prayers, and care for our brothers and sisters in Christ. After all, we are the church. We should freely lay down our lives for the cause of Christ, forget about yourself and lend a hand to help our fellow brothers and sisters in Christ.

58. - 1 Peter 4:8

"Above all, love each other deeply, because love covers over a multitude of sins."

"Above all" means more so than anything else; most important of all; before everything else; above and beyond all other consideration. So, above all, we love should each other deeply. We are to love each other profoundly, earnestly, powerfully, passionately, absolutely. Deep love is referred to as unconditional love. To love deeply calls us to love others in the same way that God loves us. This type of love will have you loving others regardless of their actions. It will cause you to forgive those who have wronged you and you will desire to seek their well-being above your own desires.

The Bible tells us that "hatred stirreth up strifes, but love covers all sins" (Proverbs 10:12). "To cover" is to put something on top of or in front of something, especially in order to protect or conceal it, but in Hebrew "to cover" means to "forgive." When you give love to another, this love shall cover or hide a great many imperfections, that you shall not notice them. When you are under the influence of love, their faults or imperfections shall be unobserved or forgiven.

So for someone to love others, this love will not allow themselves to see the wrongs done to them, because love forgives and it covers a multitude of sins, however many wrongs there may be. Yes, we will make mistakes even when we mean well, but true love means forgiving, because love covers a multitude of sins. When you love someone truly, you become blind to their faults and do not see the imperfections of those you love. Love covers, love excuses, and love forgives others, including mistakes and faults.

59. - Ephesians 4:2

"Be completely humble and gentle; be patient, bearing with one another in love."

Being humble is the practice of meekness, obedience to God, respect of self and others, submissiveness and modesty. A humble person is not proud and does not believe that they are better than other people.

To be gentle is having or showing a mild, kind, or tender temperament or character. You are careful not to upset someone or hurt them. Being gentle is the opposite of being cruel, harsh or violent. You are kind and careful about how you behave.

When you are patient you are able to remain calm and not become annoyed when waiting a long time or when dealing with problems and difficult people and circumstances. When you are patient you are able to accept or tolerate delays, problems or suffering without becoming annoyed or anxious.

The three qualities of being humble, gentle, and patient, they all correspond with the principle of love that is worked out in various of forms. Humble is mostly gentle and it is a fruit of humility that has the absence of self-assertion. Gentle is a quiet virtue, because it is by the daily quiet virtues of life that the Christian will have the spirit of forgiveness. Patient is the quality of patience,

and it is presented as either forbearance or endurance. But these three, humble, gentle, and patient are the uniting bond of love. Bearing with one another in love, is overlooking the infirmities of one another, forgiving injuries done, sympathizing with others and helping others that are in distress. Because love is the bond of perfectness. Love never seeks revenge or resentment or ill-will toward anyone. When there is love, love goes into action and it moves, influence, and engage to such a conduct that it is far more reaching and consistent that it forbear one another that suffers, that you must react in love.

60. - Proverbs 8:17

"I love those who love me, and those who seek me find me."

Love attracts love. Those who loves God and pursue wisdom will be rewarded. Our lives should be God-centered. Our minds should be saturated with God's Word (the Bible), so that we can live and walk wisely in glorifying God. We should love God with sincere affection and above all others or things in this world. We should love Jesus with all of our hearts, minds, and soul. It is through the redemption of Christ's precious blood and the riches of His grace that we have been saved. Those that loves Jesus, have His love in their hearts, and are happy. They shall be happy in the grace of God. They shall be happy in the glory of God.

Those that seek Him with sincere affection and with great diligence will find Him. Those that loves Christ have been born again and they have a spiritual knowledge of Him, and they indulge in a sweet communion with Him. They have an honest desire to be in His presence and delight in Him. Those who seek Him, places Him first place in their life, above all other things, and it is done with great eagerness, earnestness, and diligence. When you find Christ you find life, righteousness, and salvation in Him.

61. - Proverbs 10:12

"Hatred stirs up dissension, but love covers over all wrongs."

Hatred means to feel strong emotional dislike toward something or someone. Hatred is often associated with intense feelings of anger, contempt, and disgust. Hatred is sometimes seen as the opposite of love. Hatred keeps alive the old feeling of revenge and it seeks many opportunities of satisfying it. Hatred is and of itself, evil. When someone has hatred in their hearts, strife and discord is not far behind.

A dissension is a disagreement, or difference of opinion. Some common synonyms for dissension are discord, conflict, strife, disharmony, quarrel, infighting, war. There is often dissension between labor unions and governments vying for funds, or even between siblings vying for attention. As Christians we must be on guard against people who cause dissension, because without unity in serving Christ we cannot grow if someone is trying to destroy that unity.

But love covers over all wrongs. When you truly love someone, you are willing to overlook their faults and mistakes. This kind of love is selfless and self-giving. Love is the great peace maker. Those offenses within a relationship which causes discord, love will excuse them. Love has the power to cover all wrong doings by pro-

moting forgiveness and grace. We have been forgiven by Christ and we should pass that forgiveness to others. We are called to follow Jesus' example by forgiving others and overlooking others mistakes.

62. - Romans 13:8

"Owe no man any thing, but to love one another: for he that love another hath fulfilled the law."

Owe no one anything. The word "owe" means the need to pay or give something to someone because they have lent you money, or in exchange for something they have done something for you. God tells us to give to everyone what you owe them. If you owe taxes, pay your taxes. Pay to all what is owed to them. Let no debt remain outstanding, except the continuing debt to love.

Love is not an emotion that we indulge in as we please. It does not select its things, items or its objects according to their lovability. We are bound to love. We are to mirror the love Christ has for us. We are to love God with every ounce of our being. We are supposed to love our enemies and forgive them. We are supposed to love our neighbors just as we love ourselves. Every person is our creditor for the debt of love. The other person is considered a creditor and they cannot get what is due to them unless they receive the debt of love. You may payoff your mortgage, payoff your car, or even payoff your credit cards debt, thereby becoming debt free. This debt of love is never paid-off or can never be discharged.

63. - Hebrews 12:6

"Because the Lord disciplines those he loves, and he punishes everyone he accepts as a son."

Discipline is the practice of training people to obey rules or a code of behavior, using punishment to correct disobedience. No one enjoys being disciplined. Discipline is a very valuable gift that is often looked upon with disgust and disdain. God sends trials to those that He loves. He doesn't send undeserved chastisements for the purpose of inflicting pain on us. His chastisement shows that He has a paternal care for us. I have seen God's hand of discipline at work throughout my lifetime. Sometimes His hand of discipline has been misunderstood and I did slightly become upset or angry, because of what I was going through, then there were other times the Lord has allowed me to see Him working and He had allowed me to patiently endure His discipline in my life.

Many people go through a season of discipline and they draw a conclusion that God is paying them back for something they have done. Absolutely not, nothing could be further from the truth. God gave His Son, Jesus Christ to die on the cross for our sins, the punishment that was rightly due to you and me. God does not neglect us and He is very concern about us. He corrects

us and shows us that He has great love for us. If He did not love us, He would let us go about doing whatever we wanted to do thereby leaving us to pursue a course of sin that will eventually lead to disaster.

So when you are going through hardships, but have no understanding of the sovereignty of Almighty God, then your struggles may seem meaningless, pointless, and without purpose. Sometimes we often may ask ourselves, "What have I done to deserve this punishment?" We become so focused on the discomfort and the struggle, that our mindset is not on the fact that God is at work in our lives. The Lord's hand of discipline is used to train us in godliness and it keeps us from straying away from God's will for our lives. We may not understand the "why" of what we are going through, but Scripture reminds us that "All things work together for good to them that love God, to them who are the called according to his purpose" (Romans 8:28). And in the life of every child of God, whenever something deserves correcting, God disciplines those that He loves.

64. - 1 Corinthians 16:14

"Do everything in love."

All that you do, do it with love. Love should regulate all that you do for God and for others. It is all about active love. Those who actively love typically express their feelings of love freely, and willingly reveal their emotions. God has shown us that He loves us deliberately and vigorously. Therefore, God actively loves us, and calls us to actively love others. Active love seeks to be right with God and with others. Love is just not an emotion, but it is an active choice, a deliberate decision to display the heart of God that is in all believers. The command to love is at the heart of what it means to be a Christian. One of the greatest commandments is that we love God and others. Throughout Scripture there are consistent messages that believers are called to live a life marked by love.

Love should motivate everything we do. When we do everything in love, we can walk in the ways that are pleasing to God. This is a command of God and you are being obedient to God when you do everything in love. God has called us to love, and love may look different every day and each season of your life, but we can love because God loved us first. When we as believers demonstrates Christian love, it distinguishes us from the rest

of the world. When you do everything in love, love guides your thoughts, your actions, and your words. Love should be the motivator for all things.

65. - John 14:15

"If you love me, you will obey what I command."

Jesus tells us that if we love Him, then we should obey what He commands. The first word we see is the word "IF." "If" is the word that changes all things for all people. "If" means that you must show something to answer the question. The question is, "If you love Jesus you will OBEY what He commands. Do you remember the bumper sticker that read, "God is my co-pilot?" If God is your co-pilot that means that He is in the passenger's seat and your are in the driver's seat, so that means that you are first and He is second. If you love Jesus then you will allow Him to lead you, but so many people are not allowing God to lead them and they place Him, not at the Head of their lives, but He is placed somewhere else in the equation of their life, thinking that as long that He is somewhere in their life that Jesus will see it as love. You just can't place Jesus somewhere in your life, He must be at the very center of you life, the Head controlling everything. So "if" you love Jesus, claimed Him as your Lord and Savior, placed Him as the Head of your life, then you have satisfied the "if." Then you will obey what he has commanded.

Then what are His commands? They are those He spoke so plain and simple about in the Bible. Jesus' commands are Jesus

Himself. Jesus is our Moral Teacher and He simply says "Copy Me." He says "Take my yoke upon you and learn from me, for I am gentle and humble in heart" (Matthew 11:29a). His commands are Himself and they are the sum of His total perfect character, with full submission to the Father, and giving Himself entirely away to us believers. Keeping His commands is the only proper evidence of love for Jesus, because a mere profession of faith with no action, is really no real proof of love, but your love for Jesus will lead you to do His will. Love is the foundation of obedience and obedience is the result of love.

66. - Ephesians 5:2

"And live a life of love, just as Christ loved us and gave himself up for us as a fragrant offering and sacrifice to God."

We as believers in Jesus Christ, we should walk in love toward each other. We have the perfect example, Jesus, who loved us so very much that He gave Himself for us as a sacrificial lamb. His love was a sacrificial love and His sacrifice was acceptable to God, the Father. We are to follow the examples of Jesus in that special exhibition of love. We are to be imitators of God. We must imitate His walk, His actions. We must be willing to do those things that He would do. We must act the way that Jesus would act, including showing mercy. He suffered for us and He sacrificed His life for us, all because He loved us. If you desire to imitate God, then you must LOVE. You must be willing to live a life that demonstrates God's love This type of life is self-giving and it asks for nothing in return. Our walk should be a walk of love, not just with lip service, but it must be exercised, and it must all be done for Christ Jesus.

Jesus gave Himself as an offering and sacrifice to God. An "offering" is something offered, especially as a gift or contribution. Sacrifice means to make an offering of; to consecrate or present to a divinity by way of expiation or propitiation, or as a

token acknowledgment or thanksgiving; to immolate on the altar of God, in order to atone for sin, to procure favor, or to express thankfulness. So Jesus made Himself "an offering" in obedience, to do the will of God, and gave Himself as a "sacrifice," as an offering by shedding His blood on the cross. Jesus gave Himself for us, not the things in the world, but His chosen ones, His sheep, the church, for the purpose of an offering and a sacrifice to God, for a sweet smelling fragrant. He was an unblemished sacrifice who voluntarily offered up Himself, and He met the complete and adequate demands of God's justice to wipe away our sins.

67. - Proverbs 3:3-4

"Let love and faithfulness never leave you: bind them around your neck, write them on the tablet of your heart. Then you will win favor and a good name in the sight of God and man."

Love involves compassion, care, affection, and self-sacrifice. Love is a decision to compassionately, righteously, and responsibly seek the best and wellbeing of another. We should never stop living a life of love towards God, and never seek to stop caring, loving, showing mercy and kindness to others.

Faithfulness is to be true, loyal, devoted, unwavering, and steadfast. Faithfulness is very important to God and it is listed as one of the fruit of the Spirit in Galatians chapter 5. It is one of the key defining qualities of God's character, because God is completely and totally faithful. God will never break a promise. God can never act against His own character. HIs faithfulness is pure and true.

We are told to write love and faithfulness on the tablet of our hearts. When someone tells you to write something down, they are telling you to write it down so that you will not forget it. It is not enough to read God's Word and memorize it, but we are to plant His Word in our hearts and inscribe His Word of wisdom

upon the tablet of our conscience, because the Bible is God's written Word. When you are reading it, you are hearing God talking to you.

Favor is something done or granted out of goodwill, rather than from justice or for remuneration. Favor is the grace of God in our lives. The definition of grace is the unmerited favor of God, and favor means acceptance, goodwill, preferential treatment. There is nothing you can do to earn favor. Favor is the result of an attitude of love and actions of faithfulness. Favor is when God begins to bless you. When you are loving, kind, and faithful, then you will gain favor and a good name in the sight of God and man.

68. - 1 Corinthians 13:8

"Love never fails. But where there are prophecies, they will cease; where there are tongues, they will be stilled; where there is knowledge, it will pass away."

LOVE has been the inspiration for many songs, poetry, some unbelievable acts of kindness, and some life changing events. God greatest gift to us is love. We should never underestimate God's love. You can be blessed with all kinds of gifts and talents, but none of them could ever be more rewarding or more special than love. You could have all the money in the world, with all its worldly possessions, but without love a persons life means absolutely nothing.

We are reminded that all things will fail. No matter what you may accomplish, no matter how successful you may become, if you leave out love, it all doesn't mean anything. When everything else fails, love never fails. Prophecies, tongues and knowledge will all go away, but what will last? LOVE!

Love, from God flows to mankind, and love from mankind flows to God. This love is received into the heart simply by faith in Jesus Christ. This love will never fail, and it endure all things, and hope in all things, this love to us which streams from a great river of love is from God. Love accompanies us and prepares us

for eternity. Love is valuable and it is permanent because it will always exist.

69. - Matthew 22:37-39

"Jesus replied: 'Love the Lord your God with all your heart and with all your soul and with all your mind.' This is the first and greatest commandment. And the second is like it: Love your neighbor as yourself."

This is the 1st. and 2nd. greatest commandments, "to love the Lord your God with all your heart, and with all your soul and with all your mind," then "to love your neighbor as yourself." God wants us to love Him supremely, with ALL our heart, soul, and mind. As believers we should, but do we truly love Him with ALL our heart, soul, and mind? God desires so much more than our religious acts, or our money, or our good works. He desires for us to love Him more than anyone or anything. He wants our complete and total devotion. This commandment by God is the highest and most important commandment, because when we love God with all our heart, soul and mind, we will have no problem keeping God's other commandments:

You shall have no other gods before Me.
You shall not make for yourself a carved image.
You shall not take the name of the Lord your God in vain.
Remember the Sabbath day, to keep it holy.

Honor your father and mother.

You shall not murder.

You shall not commit adultery.

You shall not steal.

You shall not bear false witness against your neighbor.

You shall not covet.

To love God completely, totally, with ALL of your heart, soul, and mind, is to love Him supremely and to love Him supremely is the greatest expression of our faith. Love will motivate us to be obedient to God. Love will motivate us to be willing to do His will. Our love for God must take priority over everything else in life. God doesn't desire part of your love, but He deserves ALL of your love. True love is a decision to sacrifice and to give unselfishly. If you love God you will give Him yourself, your time, your talent, and your money.

The 2nd. greatest commandment is to love our neighbor as yourself. We do not and can not love God if we do not love others, especially our fellow brothers and sisters in Christ. God's love commands us to love Him and others, and God has a right to demand us to love, because He is love, and we are to imitate Him. We can only love our neighbors when we love God. It is this great love of God that springs forth the deed of love for Him and others, not just the believers but all people. This love is not passive, it is active. It invokes loving-kindness that causes you to be merciful and gracious towards others.

70. - 1 Corinthians 13:2-3

"If I have the gift of prophecy and can fathom all mysteries and all knowledge, and if I have faith that can move mountains, but have not love, I am nothing. If I give all I possess to the poor and surrender my body to the flames, but have not love, I gain nothing."

What is love? It is sad to say that many people have no idea what love is or what it is about. But yet, so many people want love more than anything else in the world. Who doesn't want to love and to be loved? God is the source of and sum of true love, and God has shown and continues to show His love toward us. All throughout the Bible is a display of God's love. Why did God provide coverings for Adam and Eve after they had sinned? Because He loved them. Why did God provide a cloud by day and a fire by night for the Israelites when they left Egypt heading to the Promise Land? Because He loved them. Why was God the voice for the prophets for humanity? Because He loves people. Why did God provide His Son Jesus as the atoning sacrifice for our sins? Because He was the only One who could pay the penalty for our sins and it was done out of love.

You can have all spiritual gifts; gift of prophecy, understanding all mysteries, having all knowledge, unmovable faith, gifts

of healing, speaking in tongues, interpretation of tongues, but without love you are nothing. Imagine having the gift of tongues with the ability to speak the languages of men and of angels, but if you don't have love, you would just be making noise. You can know everything there is to know, such as prophetic mysteries and having all knowledge and intellectual certainty of knowing everything as God knows and could do everything that God can do and then to have this power to remove mountains through the act of faith, but without love, you are nothing. Apart from love, everything is nothing. Do not trust in your intellect, nor your certainty, because no great amount of knowledge nor any great miracles preformed, unless they were motivated by love, it doesn't mean anything.

You can give away all that you posses and give your own body to be burned, but without love you have gained nothing. You can exercise love outwardly through acts of generosity or though self-sacrifice, but if it was not done in love, it means nothing. Love is not just a mere action, like writing a check, volunteering, love is more than this. Imagine anything great you could possibly do, imagine the greatest imaginable manifestations of anything, if any of it was done without love it would not profit you nothing.

71. - Psalm 86:5

"You are forgiving and good, O Lord, abounding in love to all who call to you."

God who is merciful and always ready to forgive us, because of His divine character. When we go before God with our petition, in God's benevolence, in His readiness to forgive, when we are overwhelmed with our difficulties, God is our Deliverer and He is able to deliver thee from ALL things. There is forgiveness with God and He has forward it to us freely giving it to us according to the riches of His grace, no sooner that it is asked, then it has been done.

God is is exceptionally good, from whom every good and perfect gift comes, God is good and He is good to others. So when we pray, we should pray out of the depths of our soul, and we should not cease from praying, praising, and expecting God to deliver us in whatever way He choses. Let us invoke, plea and petition, our case before Jesus with earnestness. Many of us do not have our prayer answered because we do not ask or we ask with the wrong motives or we are not persistent in our petition. Please remember that we are praising and petitioning the All-Sufficient God who is able to meet every one of our needs. Jeremiah says, " Our God is able to do exceeding abundantly beyond all that we ask or think according to the power that works mightily within us" (Jeremiah 32:17).

72. - Nehemiah 1:5

"Lord, the God of heaven, the great and awesome God, who keeps his covenant of love with those who love him and keep his commandments."

God created heaven and heaven is where God, Jesus, His holy angels, and His believing children lives. God didn't create heaven just for Himself, because He didn't need it. In the Bible the word "heaven" is used in three levels. The first heaven is the sky. The second heaven is what we call outer space. The third heaven is the spiritual place where God, Jesus, angelic beings lives, and where those who are Christians go when we die. Heaven is a glorious place and where God is there is always beauty and majesty and glory.

For those that keeps God's covenant of love, those who love him and keep his commandments, God will show them mercy and will not break His covenant. The love for those that are in covenant with Jesus is shown in obedience. Jesus tells us about the new covenant, he says, "If ye love me keep my commandments" (John 14:15). If someone truly loves Jesus, then they will keep His commandments. There is a relationship of love to obedience, because obedience produces love, and love will supply the obedience that supply the motive to please God.

We must have faith in the Word of God and we must trust that God will fulfill every promise that He makes. When you have faith, you are putting your trust in God and you are truly and fully convinced that God is able to do what He has promised. We read in Hebrews that without faith it is impossible to please God. God is a God of truth and has made an agreement with those who loves Him.

73. - Romans 10:9-10

"That if you confess with your mouth, Jesus is Lord, and believe in your heart that God raised him from the dead, you will be saved. For it is with your heart that you believe and are justified, and it is with your mouth that you confess and are saved."

Faith involves believing in your heart and confessing with your mouth. The words confess and confession have in common the idea of an acknowledgement of something. It is the acknowledging or confessing of faith in God and in Christ, and acknowledging or confessing of sins before God. As a Christian we are to confess openly, declare publicly, or affirm visibly the fact that Jesus Christ is our Lord and Savior, through His work of atonement through the crucifixion and the truth that He rose from the dead (resurrection), and now sits at the right hand of our holy Father in heaven. When you acknowledge this honestly, then you will experience God's covenant relationship with forgiveness of sins. Genuine confession reflects a genuine change of mind and heart (repentance).

So if you confessed your faith in Jesus, as the Lord and Savior, and really believed in your heart that God raised Him for the dead, you shall be saved by the righteousness of Jesus. You must devote

yourself to God, with your body and soul. Your soul must believe with the heart, and your body is the confessing with the mouth. Philippians 2:11 clearly tells us, "And that every tongue should confess that Jesus Christ is Lord." When we acknowledge Him as our Savior, He has the right to rule over our soul. Once we believe and confess Jesus as our Savior, then you are saved, from sin and from hell. This is the evidence of faith, because we are declaring that we are His, and we will be ruled and saved by Him, and Him only.

74. - 1 Timothy 4:12

"Don't let anyone look down on you because you are young, but set an example for the believers in speech, in life, in love, in faith and in purity."

God doesn't care about how old you are, because He is looking for willing people to serve Him. He is looking for faithful and teachable people that God can shape to be what He wants them to be. As a believer in Jesus we should be an example. The word example means a pattern; a model, something to be copied or followed. It is something that shows what a group of things is like. An apple is a example of a fruit. Everyone is an example, whether it is good or bad, you still are an example

Here we are given five specific areas in which we should set an example: speech, life, love, faith, and purity. In speech, you must control your tongue at all times. The Bible has warned us, "But I tell you that men will have to give account on the day of judgement for every careless word they have spoken. For by your words you will be acquitted, and by your words you will be condemned" (Matthew 12:36-37).

We are to be an example in life. This is about your conduct in life, the way you behave. If you are a Christian then you need to

act like it. You are to demonstrate at all times that you are a follower of Jesus and that you are living for Him.

We are to be an example in love. Love is a powerful thing. Love is the strongest power in the whole world. You should be a living example of pure Christian love. God is love and because of His love, He has provided us with our salvation. We are commanded to love one another. The Bible tells us, "If anyone says, 'I love God,' yet hates his brother, whom he has seen, cannot love God, whom he has not seen" (1 John 4:20).

We are to be an example in faith. Faith is to have great trust or confidence in something or someone. Biblical, faith is considered a belief and trust in God based on evidence but without total proof. We are to be an example of living a faithful Christian life. "But without faith it is impossible to please God, because anyone who comes to him must believe that he exists and that he rewards those who earnestly seek him" (Hebrews 11:6).

We are to be an example in purity. The meaning of purity is the quality or state of being pure. In the Bible purity is related to guiltless, blameless, or innocent behavior. Purity is freedom from anything that contaminates. Purity is the quality of being faultless, uncompromised, or unadulterated. Purity is freedom from immortality. As believers, we are to live a just and honest life. We are to be a pattern, a model, a copy of Jesus.

75. - 2 Timothy 1:7

"For God did not give us a spirit of timidity, but a spirit of power, of love and of self-discipline."

Timidity is fear of the unknown or unfamiliar or fear of making decisions and changes. The spirit of timidity means the lack of mental or moral strength, cowardice, or timidity. A person with a spirit of fear will shy away from proclaiming the gospel. Fear opens the door to the devil and fear is connected to the lack of power, lack of love, and or possibly mental problems. Fear is of the devil and it doesn't have to be rational. The devil would like to trick us into believing that fear is nothing more than an emotion, but fear must be dealt with supernaturally. The emotion of fear is nothing more than a manifestation of the spirit of fear. When fear takes over, doing the work of God takes a backseat. When doing the work for the kingdom of God, we should do it with courage and boldness. Timidity is not a character trait of God, God is not shy, fearful, afraid or timid about anything, and as His children, we shouldn't be either. The Word of God breaks the spirit of fear. Faith comes by hearing, and hearing by the Word of God. When faith comes, fear leaves with haste. In the Word of God there is power, love, faith, and mental stability. Now do not get me wrong, as a believer there will be some internal struggles, but you must

not focus on your own abilities alone, but God's abilities, then you will be filled with the Spirit of God.

The Spirit of power is the Holy Spirit. Power is a Spirit. The Holy Spirit was given to believers as a gift. The Holy Spirit is a divine person. He is the third person of the Trinity. The Holy Spirit ministers to believers in so many ways. He dwells in every believer of Christ. Every believer are the temple or dwelling place of the Spirit of God. He unites each believer in the Spirit with God, and with other believers. He intercedes for the believer. This powerful Intercessor prays for us according to God's will. He guides each believer. The Holy Spirit helps us to walk in power and not confusion. He guides us to the place of power, the perfect will of God. He imparts the love of Christ to the believer. He reveals the Biblical truth to the believer. Powerful spiritual revelation are revealed through the Holy Spirit. He comforts the believer. He comforts us in times of grief. He helps conforms the believer into the image of Jesus. He teaches us and imparts spiritual knowledge. He inspires us to true worship. He quickens us, because the same power that raised Jesus from the dead is at work in every believer. He sanctify us. We do not have to try to live holy through self effort. The power of the Holy Spirit sanctifies our thoughts and actions. He convicts us of wrongdoings. He convicts us when we are wrong and leads us to repentance. He gives assurance of salvation. He assures your position in God. He demonstrates God's power. He enables the demonstration of God's power in every area of our lives.

The spirit of love is the supernatural love of God by the Holy Spirit. God is love and His love cannot change because He never changes. To have love and to love is made possible through the

Holy Spirit. The Holy Spirit gives us the fruit of love as we keep our focus on Jesus. He allows us to love in a way that Christ loves and to love one another. Jesus has told us, "A new commandment I give to you that you love one another as I have loved you, so you must love one another" (John 13:34). Through the act of love, the Holy Spirit empowers us to demonstrate our love to others by helping them emotionally, physically, socially, mentally, and spiritually. The Holy Spirit convicts you whenever you fail to love, as you would have others to love you. He encourages us to bear-up under difficulties. He urges us to urge onward when we feel like giving up. He directs us to speak words of power and hope. He directs our minds to things above rather than problems on earth.

The spirit of self-discipline is the control the believer must exercise over their lives; the ability to control one's feelings and overcome one's weaknesses; the ability to pursue what one thinks is right, despite temptations to abandon it. Self-discipline helps us to resist temptation and avoid conforming to the things of this world. Self-discipline and self-control are not the same. Self-control is discipline in the face of pressure from an immediate urge, desire or compulsion. Self-control relates to delaying immediate gratification of the sense. Self-discipline means to exercise power over one's self. The Holy Spirit works in the believer to give them the power or strength to fight the fight of God. He gives us power, not only to patiently endure, but the power of steadfastness in resisting temptation. There must be self-discipline in your life, because if there is no discipline from yourself, then God Himself will discipline you.

76. - Psalm 33:5

"The Lord loves righteousness and justice; the earth is full of his unfailing love."

Righteousness is the quality of being morally right or justifiable; it is the quality of being right in the eyes of God, including character (nature), conscience (attitude), conduct (action), and command (word). Justice is the ethical, philosophical idea that people are to be treated impartially, fairly, properly, and reasonably by the law and by arbiters of the law, that laws are to ensure that no harm befalls another, and that, where harm is alleged, a remedial action is taken - both the accuser and the accused receive a morally right consequence merited by their actions. Biblical justice requires that every person be treated according to the same standards and with the same respect, regardless of class, race, ethnicity, nationality, gender, or any other social category.

God loves righteousness and justice. He delights in administering righteousness and justice Himself and He is pleased when acts of righteousness and justice are done by others. God is perfectly righteous and God is just. This express God's character, what He will do, because God will always do the right thing.

The earth is full of his unfailing love, because there is not a spot on earth where you cannot see God's love. Everyday, every

sunrise, and sunset, we see the manifestation of God's love. We see His love through every creation. God's love holds together the earth and His love sustains all people. His unfailing love orchestrates and control every aspect of our lives.

77. - Colossians 2:2

"My goal is that they may be encouraged in heart and united in love, so that they may have the full riches of complete understanding, in order that they may know the mystery of God, namely Christ."

The Apostle Paul's goal was that the church of Colosse would make Jesus their number one priority and to live their lives of faith in Jesus first and foremost. He wanted them to be encouraged in heart and united in love. This is the same for us today. To know God and to have a personal relationship with Him is the greatest treasure of life, but this treasure is not found through intellect, but only by our spirit, through the Holy Spirit.

We are supposed to be rooted and grounded in love for Christian knowledge of our personal Savior, Jesus Christ, so that we may know the mystery of God, namely Christ. For so many people, God is a complete mystery. Although the Bible confirms that God is indeed a mystery. The word mystery is defined as something that is difficult or impossible to understand or explain. We should have a full knowledge of the mystery of God, namely Christ. This mystery which is Christ, is in you. Christ is the mystery of God. In Him is hidden treasures of wisdom and knowledge and it is revealed to us. The treasures are found in the doctrine of the "Word of God." The Holy Spirit reveals God's knowledge of Himself to us.

When we believe in our hearts and confess with our mouth Jesus is Lord, knowledge and faith makes our soul rich. The treasures of wisdom are hid in our hearts for us in Christ. If we hear God's words with our hearts, by which He imparts Christ's nature to us, we then can retain them and live by them. Through God's Spirit which is the Holy Spirit, His Spirit reveals to us more of His words, meaning more of Himself, by this He makes His home in our hearts.

78. - Psalm 40:11

"Do not withhold your mercy from me, Lord; may your love and faithfulness always protect me."

Mercy is the compassionate treatment of those in distress, especially when it is within someone's power to punish or harm. Mercy appears in the Bible as it is related to forgiveness or withholding punishment. Mercy is a characteristic of God. God's mercy means His compassion and His kindness to us. God's mercy is rooted in His love for us. Mercy is a feeling God has for us, but also there is power in His mercy. Scripture tells us that He gives us new mercy everyday of our lives and His mercy is unchangeable.

When reflecting over our lives, especially before we became Christians, we can see how sinful we have been and how far we were from God. Our awareness of God's love for us have made us acutely aware of our sins and God's acts of loving-kindness. What God has done in the past are His wondrous deeds or miracles. What God will do in the future is called His wonderful plans; therefore, God's plans are future miracles. Since God is faithful, we can be sure that He will never change, because He is the same yesterday, as today, and will be forevermore. We are continually being preserved by the grace of God. God will always continue to be God and we should continue to recognize Him as the only true

God that is full of love and always faithful. What a joy in knowing htat we have the assurances of God, that as His children, no matter what we may face in life, God will always be with us and will protect us.

79. - Joel 2:13

"Rend your heart and not your garments. Return to the Lord your God, for he is gracious and compassionate, slow to anger and abounding in love, and he relents from sending calamity.

In the Bible days, people expressed sorrow by tearing (rending) their clothes. Anyone that saw them knew that they were grieving. If someone wanted to demonstrate their repentance and sorrow over their sin, they would publicly tear their clothes. Rend your heart and not your garments is really not your garments only, but rend your hearts rather than your garments to set the truth of repentance in what is inward, rather than outward. Empty your heart and soul of its sins and its love for sin about anything that grieves the Holy Spirit. That thing should be cut from the heart and you should return to the Lord your God. Why? Because He is gracious and compassionate, slow to anger and abounding in love, and he relents from sending calamity. As a believer in Christ, we need to understand that our time of repentance is also running out, "like sands through the hourglass, so are the days of our lives." Our lives are but specks of dust falling through the fingers of time. We do not know when our time of repentance will be up so we must repent for any wrongdoing that might be in our lives.

God is very gracious and very compassionate, very slow to anger, and abounding in love. When you turn unto the Lord God by repenting, you are keeping hope alive, as you look to God as your God, for He has promised to show us mercy when we repent and turn to Him.

God is gracious. Gracious means kind, merciful and forgiving. Gracious is the adjective from Grace. Grace is God's undeserved favor. Grace cannot be earned, it is something that God freely gives. Grace is a part of God's character.

God is compassionate. Compassion means recognizing the suffering of others and then taking action to help. It is an expression of love for those who are suffering or in need. His compassion is infinite and eternal. God's compassion is freely and tenderly given to us like a parent's compassion for their child(ren).

God is slow to anger. If someone is slow to anger they do not become angry easily. They are not easily provoked and generally demonstrate a high level of self-control. God has spared many and still spares while He waits purposely that you and I might repent and turn from your old lives and live. God's anger is an expression for His justice, and His love for us. But He is slow to anger, which means that He give people a lot of time to change.

God is abounding in love. Abounding in love means to super-abound (in quantity or quality), be in excess, be superfluous; be the better, enough and to spare, exceed, excel, increase, be left, redound, remain (over and above). God's love is inexhaustible, but reliable and indestructible.

God relents from sending calamity. The word "relent" means agreeing to something finally after initiating refusing. It also means a softening of attitude. There are two ways in the Bible that

portrays God as relenting or changing His mind. First, He relents from an intended good action; and second, He relents from intended vengeance. In 2 Samuel 24, the Lord God became angry with King David when he took a census of all the tribes of Israel and Judah. The Lord gave David three options of punishment and David chose a three days plague on Israel. Seventy thousand people died and when the Lord sent the destroying angel to destroy Jerusalem, but when the angel stretched out his hand to destroy Jerusalem, the Lord was grieved because of the calamity and said, "Enough! Withdraw your hand." The angel of the Lord was then at the threshing floor of Araunah the Jebusite. God is omniscient, that means He knows everything and He knows everything about us. God's plans are perfect and He is never ever surprised about anything.

80. - Psalm 115:1

"Not to us, Lord, not to us but to your name be the glory, because of your love and faithfulness.

When you used the word "glory" as a verb, it means to put confidence in and boast about or praise something. This may be used in the sense of glorifying God or Christ, which the Bible portrays as a good thing, but to glory in yourself is portrayed as sinful. Glory is an attribute. The most common use of the word "glory" is to describe the splendor, holiness, and majesty of God. Glory is used to describe the manifestation of God's presence as perceived by humans. God is the most glorious being in existence.

God deserves ALL the praise and ALL the glory at ALL times. God deserves the glory because of His Character. God alone lives in the realm of absolute sovereignty. We need to connect to God who is the real source of power. It is from God that power flows. It is when we are connected to Him that all things can become possible. When we are connected to God the energy flows from Him, and through our relationships.

God is love and this is His nature. It is this love of God that established His church. There is only one Love in the universe that has what it takes to meet this love-starved world and it is the love of God. There is no limit to God's love. Paul tells us, "I pray that you may be able to feel and understand how long, how wide,

how deep and how high His love really is and to experience this love for yourself" (Ephesian 3:18-19).

We glorify God because of His faithfulness. Over and over again the Bible tells us about God's faithfulness. He consistently provides for us, protects us, guides us, and He keeps His promises to us. No matter what challenges that are brought before us, through it all God has and can help us through every obstacle. And you can be confident that He will continue to keep you under His wings of protection.

81. - Mark 12:33

"To love him with all your heart, with all your understanding and with all your strength, and to love your neighbor as yourself is more important than all burnt offerings and sacrifices."

Love is defined as unselfish loyal and benevolent concern for the good of another. When you love someone with all of your heart, you make them a priority in your life. You will give them your time, your talent, your energy, and your resources.

Christ has shown us that He loves us. How did He do that? He laid down His life for us. He knows everyone's strengths and weaknesses. He is our master teacher and He has provided us with His Word (the Bible) and the Holy Spirit to guide us and teach us in the ways of truth and righteousness.

Jesus gave us two commandments about love and He linked them together. These two commandments that Jesus chose as the greatest commandments, have to do with the heart. It is linked with love and with your attitude toward God and to your neighbor. After all love caused Jesus to die on the cross in our place for our sins, because there was no other way for us to be reconciled to God. Because of what Jesus did on the cross, dying for our sins, it gives us victory over death, sin, and the devil, and it opens a new

life thereby causing us to have a new relationship with God. Our salvation is assured and God's love is unconditional. Love is the key.

We are to love God with all of our hearts. How do we do this? Jesus said, "If ye love me, keep my commandments" (John 14:15). When you love God with all of your heart, you will use your time, your energy, your talents, and your resources to keep His commandments.

82. - 2 Timothy 2:22

"Flee the evil desires of youth and pursue righteousness, faith, love and peace, along with those who call on the Lord out of a pure heart."

The word "flee" is a present tense imperative which requires continuous action on our part. We must continuously flee from the passions of our youth that pulled us away from God. We are to run away as fast we can from our youthful lusts, always saying NO to them, and avoiding situations where we can be tempted to sin. Youthful lusts can include temptations that involve sexual allurement, pride, greed, carnal pleasures, worldly attainments, and the list can go on and on.

Evil means something that is wicked, depraved or immoral. Desire is a feeling of wanting to have something or wishing for something to happen. An "evil desire" is any desire that stems from the flesh, which is the sinful nature. If you give yourself to Christ by submitting entirely to God, there is little of no time left for evil desires.

The word "pursue" means to pursue something, to do something, or try to achieve something over a period of time to pursue a goal/an aim/an objective. We are to pursue what is Pure and follow righteousness, faith, love and peace, along with those who call

on the Lord out of a pure heart. We are to pursue righteousness, which is integrity, virtue, purity of life, uprightness, correctness in thinking, feeling, and acting. Righteousness is worth pursuing and when you have it, it will change your entire life.

We are to pursue faith and the instructions concerning the necessity of faith. This is simply trusting in God. The only way to grow your faith is by getting into the Word of God. God's Word clearly tells us, "So then faith cometh by hearing, and hearing by the word of God" (Romans 10:17).

We are to pursue love. Agape love is a sacrificial love, the kind that God has for us. We must think biblical love, Christ-like, sacrificial love, because it is worth pursuing. To pursue love is to act with intention and purpose. It means to love for the sake of loving, with no expectations of something in return.

We are to pursue peace. Peace is a stress-free state of security and calmness that comes when there is no fighting or war, everything coexisting in perfect harmony and freedom. The Hebrew word "peace" is shalom. Shalom peace is the result of right relationships with God, one another, and with creation. God is our Source of peace. We are to pursue peace between individuals, as well as harmony with all people.

We are to pursue righteousness, faith, love, and peace "with those who call on the Lord out of a pure heart." We are to find those who are "purposeful" and pursue godliness, because you should not have to do it alone. We all need good friends who can join us in our fleeing and pursuing. These friends are characterized by two qualities - prayer and purity. I am talking about godly friends, those that you know are in the will of our heavenly Father. Those friends that are living a spirit-filled purposeful life, pursuing godliness. The reason you will need friends, because you cannot do it on your own. Fleeing temptation is exhausting and you will need much encouragement. Pursuing godliness can be difficult and you will need some support. It is true that God is always with you, but human companionship is also essential.

83. - Psalm 62:12

"Also to You, O Lord, belong mercy and lovingkindness, for You render to every man according to his work."

God is merciful and full of lovingkindness. Grace is getting what you don't deserve, mercy is not getting what you do deserve. God's mercy is another expression of His love. God's mercy is an expression of His love for us and His greatest mercy is the forgiveness of our sins. Our sin debt was paid through the mercy of God through His Son Jesus Christ. God's mercy means His pity, compassion, and kindness toward us. God is the Father of mercies and the God of all consolation and hope. We should always place our trust in Him, because we as human beings are sinful and unworthy, though we deserve nothing but His wrath, yet because of who He is, we receive all good things because of His mercy.

Lovingkindness is a tender and benevolent affection. God's lovingkindness is His faithful love in action that is expressed in His relationship with us. His persistent and unconditional tenderness, kindness, and mercy, a relationship that He seeks with us, with love and mercy. God's lovingkindness is expressed both through His loyalty to His covenant and His love for His people along with a faithfulness to keep His promises.

God is almighty and He can destroy all of His enemies and yours too. But, yet, He is mild and merciful, and He can pardon those people of their sins and short comings, by graciously rewarding them according to their integrity. For God renders every person according to their work, and this is a reason of proving that both power and mercy belongs to God. God has the power to punish the wicked according to their evil and sinful deeds and the mercy to reward the believers.

84. - Revelation 3:19

"Those whom I love I rebuke and discipline. So be zealous, and repent."

The word "rebuke" express sharp disapproval or criticism of someone because of their behavior or actions. In the Bible, the term "rebuke" is used to convey a strong expression of disapproval, reproof, or correction. The concept of rebuke is closely tied to discipline, correction, and the pursuit of righteousness. But rebuke is simply correction. God corrects us because it is better to obey than to disobey.

Discipline is the quality of being able to behave and work in a controlled way which involves obeying particular rules or standards. Discipline protects us from danger. Discipline helps us learn self-control and self-discipline. Discipline helps us develop a sense of responsibility. Discipline helps instill values. The Bible tells us, "Whoever loves discipline loves knowledge, but he who hates reproof is stupid" (Proverbs 12:1). Also, "For the moment all discipline seems painful rather than pleasant, but later it yields the peaceful fruit of righteousness to those who have been trained by it" (Hebrews 12:11).

So Jesus tells us that those whom He loves, He rebuke and discipline, and of course if He rebuke and discipline His children,

then they deserve it. We must understand that this is the proof of His love for us. If those that belongs to Jesus go astray, those who are disobedient, with great pain to Jesus, He administers chastisement to save those that are His. There is no greater proof of His love when He has to do this. The discipline of God is not something which we should resent, but something for which we should be devoutly thankful.

"Be zealous and repent." Zealous is the eagerness and ardent interest in pursuit of something. Zealous means to have an ardor or fervor of spirit. This change of heart and mind is only demanded in true repentance, that means turn from the error of your ways. The word "repent" means to feel or express sincere regret or remorse about one's wrongdoing or sin. We should have a zeal for God. Zeal is a burning desire to please God, to do His will, and to spread His Gospel against everything that is evil, against all false worship, all sin and iniquity. And therefore, repent. For us believers, our sin doesn't destroy our relationship with God. Sin doesn't destroy our relationship with God, but it harms our relationship with Him. When we sin and do not confess our sins, we will begin to feel a distance from God, but God pursues us by convicting us or our sin and allowing us to feel bad about our unconfessed sin. It is the unconfessed sin that harms our fellowship with God. God is the only One that is able to forgive us our our sins. He invites us to come to Him and confess our sins and when we do, He covers our sins with the blood of Jesus, His Son. When we turn from our sin and turn to Jesus, God forgives us and our fellowship with Him is restored.

85. - Psalm 57:10

"For great is your love, reaching to the heavens, your faithfulness reaches to the skies."

God's power cannot show without God's love being in place. The only way that we can see God's power is because of His love. When God created the heavens, the earth, mankind, and everything that exist, it was His power that created all things, because of the love and desire He has for His children. When Jesus died for us, God resurrected Him from the dead and that was the manifestation of God's power that came into effect because of His great love for all believers. It is the love of God that places a demand on the power of God. His love reaching to the heavens simply implies "sky high," that is something larger than we could ever imagine, because it is beyond measure.

"God's faithfulness reaches to the skies." His faithfulness is great. His faithfulness provides a way of escape from temptation. His faithfulness provides forgiveness of our sins. His faithfulness endures to all generations. God will always be faithful in His purposes and His promises. He will be faithful in performing His Gospel and the doctrines of it. We should always have a praise in our heart for God because of His boundless mercy and unfailing faithfulness.

86. - Romans 12:9

"Love must be sincere. Hate what is evil; cling to what is good."

This is what it means to live the Christian life, "Love must be sincere. Hate what is evil; cling to what is good." Being sincere is being free from pretense or deceit. Sincere is being genuine in feeling. It stresses absence of hypocrisy. Paul is describing the kind of love which is recognized as genuine. This should be a daily prescription and meditation in our thoughts as we live our lives in association with everyone. To love is to live by the Golden Rule, "So in everything, do to others what you would have them do to you" (Matthew 7:12). Christian love should be true and pure love, and it will manifest itself by showing that you love your fellow man and woman.

We should hate what is evil and cling to what is good. There should be no squabbling, no petty jealousy. No miserable strife for recognition, in which we all are some what are guilty of. There should be no lies told, but our hearts should be filled with love for one another. Our love for each other should be sincere and free from any deceit, and unmeaning deceitful comments. We must love each other and be delighted in whatever is kind and loving. We must not only do what is good and right in the eyes of

the Lord, but we must cleave to it. Everything that we do for one another is summed up unto one word, "LOVE." We must not only be kind and loving to our friends, strangers, and family, but Christians must not harbor any unkindness nor anger for their enemies.

87. - Song of Solomon 8:6

"Place me like a seal over your heart, like a seal on your arm; for love is as strong as death, its jealousy unyielding as the grave. It burns like blazing fire, like a mighty flame."

The Song of Solomon book reveals the intimate relationship God desires to have with us. Song of Solomon shows us the beauty in the exclusive relationship between a husband and a wife. It is a tribute to the joys of a wedded life - only they can satisfy the desire they have for each other. Intimacy within a marriage has been ordained by God.

Solomon's wife wants him to set her as a seal on his heart and his arm, in order to demonstrate that both his love and his strength truly belongs to her. Her reasoning for this is because of her unquenchable and intense love for him, and the opposite of love - jealousy. Her love for Solomon is so great that she could not bear the thought of being without him.

Her love was so great for him that it was as strong as death. Today in our wedding vows we say, "I [name] take you [name] to be my wife/husband, to have and to hold from this day forward, for better, for worse, for richer, for poorer, in sickness and in health, to love and to cherish, **till death do us part**, according to God's holy law. In the presence of God I make this vow." All those

that love knows that death will bring a separation that will give rise to such great pain and much grief. Those who are believers in Christ long and hope that God, in His great mercy will enable us to be together in eternity. But in spite of our deep love for our love one, physical death is a reality.

"It burns like blazing fire, like a mighty flame." What a strange comparison between love and fire. Love and jealousy are both emotions, but some people who love someone can get jealous, but jealousy is an escalation of a person's insecurities. Jealousy is a fear of losing your partner. Jealousy is as cruel as the grave and it never lets anyone go. To be consumed by jealousy like that is heartless and unyielding. But loves strikes like lightning, like the very flame of God and it is powerful. For true love is so very important and priceless.

88. - Romans 13:10

"Love does no harm to its neighbor. Therefore love is the fulfillment of the law"

Love would seek to do good and it does not harm anyone. Love seeks justice, truth, and benevolence. Love does not slander, it does not cheat, nor commit fraud, nor permit schemes of dishonesty. Love doesn't seek any ill will, therefore love is the fulfillment of the law, meaning that all the Law requires us is to do is to"LOVE" others. The law of God requires us to do justice and observe truth. If you truly love others, all the demands of the Law would be satisfied. When we love others in the same way that Jesus loves us, we fulfill God's law, "for love is the fulfillment of the law." The basic principles of Christian living are to love others and to live righteously. Loving others is an obligation. Loving others is what God requires of us.

89. - Proverbs 17:17

"A friend loves at all times, and a brother is born for adversity."

Afriend is someone that you experience a bond with. A friend is someone you trust and enjoy being around and you can rely on them for support. Friends are people with whom you can be yourself. When you are with them, you do not have to be on guard. You can say what you think, and you can breathe easily and freely.

A brother is born for adversity. What does this mean? Friends love through all kinds of weather and families stick together in all kinds of trouble. A friend is always a friend and families will stick together through all kinds of trouble. I have known some family members that would not stick together and be supportive and loving. But a brother is more than a friend, and he should show himself as a friend.

90. - Leviticus 19:18

"Do not seek revenge or bear a grudge against one of your people, but love your neighbor as yourself. I am the Lord."

Revenge is committing a harmful action against a person or group in response to a grievance, be it real or perceived. The Bible constantly tells us, "Dearly beloved, avenge not yourselves, but rather give place unto wrath: for it is written, Vengeance is mine; I repay, saith the Lord" (Romans 12:19).

When you hold a grudge you are harboring anger, bitterness, resentment, or harboring other negative feelings long after someone has done something to hurt you. The Bible tells us, "Let all bitterness and wrath and anger and clamor and slander be put away from you, along with all malice" (Ephesians 4:31).

"But love your neighbor as yourself." Jesus went to great lengths to define who is our neighbor. In Luke 10:29 a lawyer asked Jesus, "Who is my neighbor?," and Jesus replied by telling him the story of the Good Samaritan. The story tells about a man who was going from Jerusalem to Jericho when he was beaten and robbed and left to die. A priest and a Levite passed by him and did nothing. But a Samaritan passed by and took pity on him. He took care of his wounds, took him to an inn, and paid

his expenses. Then Jesus asks the lawyer, "Which of these three do you think was a neighbor to the man who fell into the hands of the robbers?" (Luke 10:36). The lawyer's reply, "The one who had mercy on him." A neighbor is any one we encounter who has a need. We should love our neighbors as we love ourselves, sincerely and heartily, by doing all the good to him or her as you would do for yourself.

"I am the Lord," who is the Creator of all mankind, and everything that exists. "I am the Lord," who is a God of graciousness. "I am the Lord," who is a God that is merciful. "I am the Lord," who is a God that is slow to anger. "I am the Lord," who is a God that is loving. He has commanded us to love one another, and only Him does vengeance belongs and He expects us to be obedient to Him and His laws.

91. - Romans 12:10

"Be devoted to one another in brotherly love. Honor one another above yourselves."

The meaning of "devoted" is characterized by loyalty and devotion. All of our duty towards each other is summed up in one word, "LOVE." Love is the key. We are to love others sincerely. We are to love others honestly and genuinely. We should love and delight in whatever is kind and useful. We must not only do what is good, but we must cleave to it. There isn't anything or situation that true love can't change and make it right.

God chose us out of love. Love is one of the major tasks in life. We are called to love as God loves us. He wants us to be rooted and grounded in love. We should relate to one another in love. We should always speak the truth in love. We should build up the body of Christ in love. We should walk in love. When someone interact with you, they should see in you the love of Christ and be drawn to Him.

92. - Songs of Solomon 6:7

"Many waters cannot quench love; rivers cannot wash it away. If one were to give all the wealth of his house for love, it would be utterly scorned."

True love is unquenchable. The word "unquenchable" is used for describing a feeling that is so strong that it cannot be satisfied. It is incapable of being quenched, extinguished, like an unquenchable fire or thirst. No matter the circumstances of life, the fire of love cannot be extinguished. Especially God's love, because His love is unquenchable and you cannot put it out. God's love has been proven and it is still being proven - through His Son Jesus Christ. The Bible tells us that God demonstrated His love for us, that while we were yet sinners Jesus Christ died for us.

"River cannot wash it away." When you love someone, there is nothing that you can do to stop it from being manifested. There is nothing that can stop you from demonstrating your love for someone. God's love is unquenchable and no one can stop God and nobody can stop you from loving Him. We are faced with so many temptations, distractions, and we will face so many obstacles in this life that will test our love for Jesus. But with the help of the Holy Spirit, we can resist and overcome them all, just to demonstrate the love that we profess for Him.

"If one were to give all the wealth of his house for love, it would be utterly scorned." God is Love. Love is God. When I say that God is Love, I am talking about a LOVE that operates from a place of pure, uncompromising truth. God is our Father, and God is love, and if we have love in us then our love manifests itself in a pure, uncompromising way regarding truth. The Bible is a dictionary explaining God's love. If you study God's Word, then you will come to a greater understanding of His Love. His love is greater than anything than man or woman can ever be able to give you. And if you accept His definition of His love and receive it in your life, then you are going to have an experience with God that will be absolutely glorious.

93. - Proverbs 21:21

"He who pursues righteousness and love finds life, prosperity and honor."

To pursue after righteousness and love is to follow Jesus. Righteousness is a way of life that is all about doing the right thing. Righteousness shows great concern for morals and ethnics. The word "right" in righteousness is a word about taking a stand and doing the right thing. Like trying to help the needy, the poor, and oppressed people is a cause for righteousness.

If you seek to find your life, then you will lose it. But if you seek to give your life to Christ, you will truly find it. Righteousness fused with kindness, hesed mercy, compassion, love, grace, and faithfulness. Hesed is the idea of faithful love in action. Those that pursue righteousness will receive more than they seek. The Bible clearly tells us, "But seek first his kingdom and his righteousness, and all these things will be given to you as well" (Matthew 6:33).

Those that act justly and kindly will prosper and obtain justice and honor. We should pursue righteousness, an evangelical righteousness, the righteousness of Jesus. We are to follow after it, to seek it, to desire it, and thirst after it. Then you shall obtain from God, what is right and due to you, either from God, by virtue of His gracious promise or from mankind, whose hearts God will touch to deal with you fairly, justly, and kind.

94. - Philippians 2:2

"Then make joy complete by being like-minded, having the same love, being one in spirit and purpose"

Being like-minded is having similar interests and opinions. Other words for like-minded are: agreeing, compatible, unity, in harmony, united of one mind, being on the same page, just to name a few. It is all about "unity." Unity demands that we be like minded, that we get along with each other. Unity is based on a common love and this common love is for Jesus Christ. Unity expresses itself through sharing mutual beliefs and values.

How do we achieve "unity?" Unity is being together or at one with someone or something. It is the opposite of being divided. It is a word that represents togetherness or oneness. It is the state of being in full agreement and harmony. This "oneness" is so important in the eyes of God. When you are in agreement that unity is important. Unity is achieved through humility. "Do nothing out of selfish ambition or vain conceit, but in humility consider others better than yourselves" (Philippians 2:3).

If you adopt an attitude of humility instead of self-importance, or other-centeredness of self-centeredness, of regarding the views of others of greater importance, if you avoid unfounded self-glory and glory in Jesus Christ, then you can live together in harmony.

163

95. - Galatians 5:13

"You, my brothers and sisters, were called to be free. But do not use your freedom to indulge the sinful nature; rather, serve one another in love."

"You, my brother and sisters, were called to be free." Jesus wants us to know that we were called to freedom, so do not turn your freedom into an opportunity for the flesh, but through love, by serving one another. This is the fulfillment of the Law. Remember that the Bible tells us, "You shall love your neighbor as yourself." This commandment sums up the essence of the freedom that we have in Jesus. We are set free to love and have a desire in our hearts to serve one another.

We have to look at freedom in the way God does and how God does not. When you delve into the Bible, we see a kind of freedom with an understanding of the slavery we find ourselves in, as in slavery to sin. But the only way to find real freedom from sin is by having a true and real relationship with God, through Jesus Christ. We are made free in Christ. Jesus Himself is the ultimate example to follow. He chose to lay aside His freedom, to choose the cross, which is the ultimate expression of love.

We are not to use our freedom to indulge in the flesh. We are to be aware of the natural man and its manifestation. That is living

according to the flesh. The word "flesh" depicts sinful impulses and carnal cravings. The "flesh" has its own mind and desires, so if a believer do not keep it under control, those desires will show their ugly and sinful faces. In other words, the flesh will manifest those evil and sinful desires. "The acts of the sinful nature are obvious: sexual immorality, impurity and debauchery; idolatry and witchcraft; hatred, discord, jealousy, fits of rage, selfish ambition, dissensions, factions and envy; drunkenness, orgies, and the like…" (Galatians 5:19-21).

We have freedom to serve each other in love. We are to follow the example of Jesus, there we can express our freedom to love and serve one another, because this is what we have been set free to do. When you exercise that freedom, you will find that your freedom to love will cause you to do things that you could not or would not have done on our own, but only through the love of Jesus, then you will discover that this freedom to serve one another has so many blessed benefits.

96. - 2 Corinthians 13:11

"Finally, brothers, good-bye. Aim for perfection, listen to my appeal, be of one mind, live in peace. And the God of love and peace will be with you."

This is Paul's final appear in his letter to the church in Corinth and his final appeal is a call for unity. Paul explains the nature of Christian ministry and this is an example even today, because it has much to teach us about how we should handle our ministries. Those involved in ministry should be blameless, sincere, confident, caring, open, and will to suffer for the sake of Jesus.

A formula is prescribed as we aim for perfection. We are to aim for perfection. Being perfect means being without fault or defect; flawless. Literally, it means being mature. How? Being the right examples. Having the right motives.

We should be of one mind. How? Having the same goals. Using the same holy Book (the Bible). Following, studying, and believing the same doctrines. Doctrine is scriptural teaching on theological truths. Doctrine is indispensable to Christianity. Christianity doesn't exist without it.

We are to live in peace. The word "peace" conjures up a passive picture of one showing an absence of civil disturbance or hostilities, or a personality free from internal and external strife. We are

to literally cultivate peace, in the House of God, before the eyes of mankind, and to honor God. God alone is the source of peace, for He is "Yahweh Shalom".

97. - Psalm 116:1-2

"I love the Lord, for he heard my voice; he heard my cry for mercy. Because he turned his ear to me, I will call on him as long as I live."

The Lord hears our voices when we pray and he also hears our cries for mercy. God loves us so much that He loves to listen to the words that you and I say to Him. God hears every plea and petition. He saves prayers as well as our words in a golden bowl. "Then another angel with a gold incense burner came and stood at the altar. And a great amount of incense was given to him to mix with the prayers of God's people as an offering on the gold altar before the throne. The smoke of the incense, mixed with the prayers of God's holy people, ascended up to God from the altar where the angel had poured them out" (Revelation 8:3-4).

There are benefits in serving the Lord. For the Psalmist asks, "What shall I render unto the Lord for all his benefits toward me" (Psalm 116:12-13). How can we repay the Lord for being so mighty good to us? We can't! King David wrote, "Bless the Lord, O my soul, and forget not all his benefits" (psalm 103:1). And what are some of God's benefits to us? According to the holy Bible, I will list a few:

He forgives us of all of our sins.

He keeps our feet from falling.

He ransoms us from hell.

He heals us.

He surrounds us with His lovingkindness and tender mercies

He fills our life with good things.

He gives justice to all who are mistreated.

He is merciful and tender toward those who do not deserve it.

He is slow to get angry.

He is full of kindness and love.

He never bears a grudge.

He does not remain angry with us forever.

He has not punished us as we deserve for our sins.

He has removed our sins as far away from us as the east is from the west.

He is like a father to us.

He is tender and sympathetic to those that loves Him.

The greatest benefits in life are those that comes from the goodness of God.

God will never force you to love Him, but in return of the love that He offers you, if you would allow Him to love you and if you would accept His love for you, He offers to adopt you as His child. So when you call on Him, He is very interested in what is going on in your life, He not only listens when you tell Him about your problems, but He actually does something about them.

98. - Psalm 42:8

"By day the Lord directs his love, at night his song is with me - a prayer to the God of my life."

Whatever you maybe going through, you must see God as the God of your life. Through God, we have a way of escape. To sweeten it all, God's lovingkindness is what keep us rooted and grounded. It is a lifeline when we are drowning in tribulation, despair, and trouble. Yes, the day will turn into night, figuratively and literally, but through the love of God you will receive strength. No day shall ever come that the Lord would not extend us His grace, and only He has the authority to command mercy for His chosen children.

Our God, is the God of the nights as well as the day. We as His children shall never be unprotected, whether day or night. His song shall be with us. Songs of blessings shall cheer us when we are feeling gloomy at night. No music is as sweet as praise music. Affliction may dim our candle or may even put it our, but those affliction should not silence our praises to the Lord. In Jesus we have the reason for hope especially in the days of affliction. God is our Rock and He is faithful and He will deliver. We will face all kinds of things in our lives, but God is always on our side. With God, we can overcome everything, but we must live our lives with the joy and peace of God in our hearts, and this is the hope that is afforded us by the power of the Holy Spirit.

99. - 1 John 3:17

"If anyone has material possessions and sees his brother in need but has no pity on him, how can the love of God be in him?"

To have material possessions is to own a certain amount of wealth, property, and resources. Possessions are temporal. They perish, spoil, and fade. Those who have "world goods" or "enough money to live well" should not be arrogant nor put their hope in their wealth, but should their trust and hope in God, because it is God that provides us with everything that we need and for our enjoyment.

If a person, who has something to give, sees another person in need and does not help that person, it is doubtful that the person who refuses to give has the love of God living in their heart. A person that loves God will help if they are able. When you have the love of God in your heart that love of God speaks to us out of compassion. Jesus set the standard for compassion.

Love requires more than idle talk, it demands simple acts of kindness that meet the needs of our brothers and sisters that are in distress. Our love for one another is put to the test when we do good when presented the opportunity. After all LOVE is a verb. It is something that you do. You can keep telling people that you love people, but if you can't show people your love with actions, then it is not love.

100. - Psalm 94:18

"When I said, 'My foot is slipping,' your love, O Lord, supported me."

"My foot is slipping," - Sometimes we come to a point of failing into mischief, disobedience, falling into sin, falling away from faith. You can feel your foot suddenly beginning to slip and you fell the fear and panic, and you wonder, how did I end up where I am? Sin is a slippery slope. Sometimes one little sin can lead to a bigger sin that leads to another after another. Praise be to the Lord that we serve a merciful, gracious and power God whose powerful hand can immediately stretch out His hand to support every step that we make.

It is God's pity and love for us that causes His power to give us the spiritual support that we need. We are weak and we do not have the ability to stand on our own strength and we must acknowledge it, because only God can keep our foot from slipping. It is through God's mercy that keeps us from falling.

www.ingramcontent.com/pod-product-compliance
Lightning Source LLC
Chambersburg PA
CBHW040728120726
48010CB00001B/51